The Sensory Connection

Sensory and Communication Strategies that WORK!

Nancy Kashman, BS, LOTR & **Janet Mora**, MA, CCC-SLP

Sensory RESOURCES LLC

Las Vegas

Published by:

2500 Chandler Ave., Suite 3
Las Vegas, NV 89120-4064
(702) 433-0404
(888) 357- 5867
Fax: (702) 891- 8899
E-mail: info@sensoryresources.com
www.SensoryResources.com

CIP data available from the publisher or from the Library of Congress.

Originally published in May 2002 as *An OT and SLP Team Approach: Sensory and Communication Strategies That WORK!* under ISBN 1-931615-07-1

ISBN-13: 978-1-931615-21-1
ISBN-10: 1-931615-21-7   Revised edition, June 2005

Contents

Understanding Sensory Integration & Communication   11
    A Brief Look at Sensory Integration   11
    Communication and Sensory Integration   14

Sensory Processing Difficulties   19
    Vestibular System   19
    Proprioceptive System   22
    Tactile System   24
    Auditory System   27
    Visual System   29
    Olfactory System   29
    Oral/Feeding Difficulties   30

Sensory-Based Behaviors   33
    Sensory Defensiveness   33
    Self-Abusive and Self-Stimulating Behaviors   34
    Prompt Dependency   35

Approach to Intervention   39
    Therapeutic Approach   41
    Treatment Cycle   42
    Teaming   43
    Benefits of Teaming   44

Assessment   47
    Communication   48
    Sensory Motor   50
    Environment   52
    Summary   52

The Environment   53
    Environmental Effects on Level of Arousal   53
    Environmental Strategies to Prepare for Learning   55

Additional Environmental Strategies   63
Environmental Visual Supports   68
Sensory "Cheat Sheet"   72
Case Studies   73

Intervention   77
    Treatment Strategy Guidelines
       to Facilitate Learning and Communication   78
    Vestibular Input Precautions   80
    Sensory and Communication-Based Treatment Strategies
       for Children   80

Strategies for the Adult & Older Child   105
    Proprioceptive/Vestibular   105
    Tactile   108
    Enterprise Activities   109

Transitions & Informational Tools   117
    Transitions   117
    Informational Tools   120

Oral & Feeding Interventions   125
    General Recommendations   126
    Proprioceptive/Tactile   126
    Taste Suggestions   128
    Food Suggestions for Children and Adults   129

Developing Communication Skills   131
    Individuals with Severe Difficulties   131
    Individuals with Moderate Difficulties   133
    Individuals with Mild Difficulties   134

Using Videos   141
    Guidelines for the Production of Intervention Videos   144

Teaming Case Studies   147
    The Orphanage   149
    Conclusions   150

Appendicies   151
    Sensory Integration Disorders   151
    Guide to Assessment of Environment   157
    "Stuffed Pants"   161
    "Stuffed Sweatshirt"   163
    Weighted Vests   165
    Oral Box   167
    Example of a Fact Sheet   169
    Example of a Home/Classroom Handout   173
    General Communication Tips   177
    References & Recommended Readings   179
    Recommended Assessment Sources   185
    Recommended Resources   187

Index   189

Dedication

This book is dedicated to our families without whose support we could never have completed our dream:

The Kashmans: Steve, Randi, Scott, Jennifer, Brian, Zachary, Skyler, Sydney, Monia, and Frances Palaviccini

The Moras: Arthur, Jill, James, Alyson, Jim, and Barbara Glaser

A special thank you to the Chartwell Center; Arizona Centers for Comprehensive Education and Life Skills (ACCEL); St. John the Baptist School System; Tammy Glaser, MS; Lorna Jean King, LOTR; Jennifer Kashman, LOTR; Carol Kranowitz, MA; Mindy Malik, PhD; Jean Dutro, RPT; Barbara McMasters, MEd; Wendi Sobelman, MA; Judy Beck, BA; Marilyn Schletzer; Patty Marashian, MA; our editor, Polly McGlew; our publisher, David Brown; and all our special children and their families.

Introduction

Individuals diagnosed with autism, Asperger's syndrome, PDD-NOS, and other challenges, such as cerebral palsy, Down syndrome, and attention deficit disorder, frequently exhibit not only communication difficulties but also a vast array of sensory integration issues. Any one or a combination of the senses can be affected: sight, hearing, touch, taste, smell, proprioception (sense of where one's body is in space), and balance (also called the vestibular sense).

Language and communication difficulties follow an equally diverse pattern. Some children can hardly verbalize, whereas others possess highly developed expressive language but have impairments in their functional use of speech. Whatever the combination of language and sensory challenges, these difficulties can impact widespread areas of development, including social interactions, motor skills, academics, and self-esteem.

Traditionally, speech-language pathologists (SLPs) have addressed communication difficulties, and occupational therapists (OTs) have addressed sensory integration needs. In recent years, however, therapists have paid more attention to finding effective and functional solutions to the communication and sensory difficulties these children possess. Therapists have started working as a team for the benefit of the child with autism and sensory integration disorders. This has been especially true with speech-language pathologists and occupational therapists.

Sensory integration techniques can modulate the level of arousal, thereby enhancing a person's ability to attend, function, and learn. Therapists have found that when a child is engaged in more physical activities, he responds better to efforts to elicit speech. A child often utters sounds, words, and sentences when bouncing, swinging, jumping, or running.

A team approach to working with individuals with autism spectrum disorder (ASD) and other developmental disorders involves not only the therapists, doctors, and other professionals, but also the parent/caregiver and (ideally) the individuals themselves. Teaming provides a holistic approach to facilitate skill development. Over time, teaming becomes trans-disciplinary as the interventionists assume each other's roles (when appropriate), and opportunities for learning become continuous.

The information and strategies presented in the first edition of this book, originally titled *An OT and SLP Team Approach*, were developed over a period of years. It was our hope that they would provide a functional approach to working with children and adults with autism and sensory integration dysfunction. This book continues to be a compilation of our own experiences, as well as suggestions and ideas shared by other professionals and parents. We are so thankful to the many parents and professionals who thought *An OT and SLP Team Approach* was worth acquiring and reading.

For this second edition, we have chosen to add more strategies that we developed through our work and by having so many readers share their ideas with us. We have also chosen another title, *The Sensory Connection*, that we believe better reflects the content and intent of this book. *The Sensory Connection* serves as a reminder that an individual's sensory difficulties are often the reason for his behavior. Understanding the connection between one's sensory experiences and behaviors is crucial for the development and implementation of appropriate interventions.

Within our practice and through sharing our strategies with you, our goal is to enhance the developmental skills of individuals with sensory integration dysfunction, ASD, and other diagnoses, thereby providing them with an opportunity to participate more fully in functional life tasks and experience a more positive quality of life, both now and in the future.

Chapter One

Understanding Sensory Integration
& Communication

A Brief Look at Sensory Integration

At an early age, children learn about themselves and the world around them by exploring, experiencing, and playing. With the use of their senses, and through their daily routines and interactions with others, children continuously gather, organize, and respond to information. Individuals who have sensory integration deficits may have difficulties in one or more areas of development, including communication, social interactions, academic learning, and recreational activities.

Sensory integration allows correct interpretation of experiences and appropriate responses to stimuli. It is the ability of the central nervous system to organize and process information from different sensory channels in order to produce an appropriate response.

Dr. Jean Ayres, an occupational therapist, developed the theory and treatment approach of sensory integration. This approach, which was initially used for children with learning difficulties, expanded over the years and is now used for individuals with many other diagnoses. Autism, cerebral palsy, Down syndrome, developmental delays, Alzheimer's disease, and traumatic brain injury are only some of the disabilities that may produce sensory integration difficulties.

Sensory integration is the basis for all behavior. The central nervous system takes in information and enables the brain to register, filter out irrelevant information, integrate, organize, and respond appropriately. Accurate sensory processing allows for appropriate modulation or regulation of one's level of arousal and is the glue that basically "holds it all together." Sensory integration is an important foundation, influencing the acquisition of cognition, language, motor skills, self-help skills, and social and emotional well-being, which directly affect the quality of one's behaviors and skills.

There are seven senses: Vision, smell, touch, taste, and hearing are external sources of sensory input. The vestibular and proprioceptive systems are two less-known, internal sensory sources that also provide necessary information. The vestibular system (balance) and the proprioceptive system (body awareness) provide the feelings of movement and gravity.

Sensory integration evolves along a continuum, acquired through normal development, exploration, and play. Birth through ages seven to ten years is a particularly important time of sensory motor development and exploration. However, this skill continues to develop throughout life. Although changes may occur more rapidly in the child, the plasticity of the brain allows learning to be continuous. For the older child and adult, compensatory sensory strategies potentially enable them to participate more fully in life.

When sensory integration dysfunction occurs, one cannot organize and integrate sensory input. The sensory experience is unpredictable, lacks meaning, and may affect a person quite differently from one time to another. This inconsistency places the individual in a high stress or anxiety mode—unprepared for learning new skills or participating in life tasks.

Breakdown in sensory integration may occur at various levels. Registration is the ability to perceive incoming information. This is our awareness meter, the first instant when we hear another's voice, smell cookies baking, or feel our hand against a cold tile. Difficulties occur when one is unable to adequately filter the incoming sensations and under- or overregisters sensory input. The individual who underregisters input perceives it to a lesser degree and may seek additional sensations or be unresponsive to sensory stimuli. Conversely, the individual who overregisters sensory input may present avoiding and defensive behaviors.

Sensory integration and organization is the ability to receive information from a variety of sensory systems (multichannel input), make sense of it, and organize it for use. Difficulties can occur with single or multichannel sensory input. Monochanneling refers to being only able to process one sensory channel at a time. For example, a person may be able to process visual information but cannot process auditory information at the same time. When multisensory demands are placed on this individual, sensory "jumbling" may occur.

Interestingly, individuals with adequate sensory integration turn off overwhelming multichannel input when stressed or when concentrating on a difficult task. While following directions to an unfamiliar place, the closer one gets to the destination, the more likely one is to turn the radio off in order to improve focus and decrease distractions.

Modulation is a dynamic and ongoing process. As various internal and external inputs are processed, the individual must adjust and maintain an optimum level of arousal. He must also maintain where his attention is centered.

There are varying degrees of sensory processing deficits. Within the autism spectrum, sensory processing difficulties can affect any combination of the senses in any degree of severity. Likewise, individuals with other diagnoses, such as attention deficit disorder, learning disability, Down syndrome, traumatic brain injury, and other challenges may also experience sensory integration difficulties. The etiology of the diagnoses may be different, but the presenting sensory issues are often the same.

Communication and Sensory Integration

Kevin points for what he wants, Armond prefers to write letters, Holly uses simple signing and word approximation, and Michael speaks in complete sentences. All are communicating.

Communication is the ability to exchange information and ideas within a social setting. From the time they are born, infants begin the process of learning how to communicate. They learn to communicate by hearing, seeing, touching, and moving about their world. Infants quickly make associations between their utterances, such as crying because they are wet or hungry, and achieving the desired result—a dry diaper or food.

Essential to these communications is the complex array of sensations that alerts babies to the necessity of connecting to others in their environments. From the first day of life, the accurate perception and integration of information provided by their external and internal sensory receptors give children the means to make sense of their environments. A well-integrated sensory system becomes the vehicle for nonverbal expressions such as gestures, smiles, or frowns, and later, for the production of speech and language. Children who experience difficulty integrating and interpreting a world full of sensations will have difficulty learning how to communicate. Without adequate processing of internal and external sensory cues, children with sensory integration dysfunction lag behind in their early communication attempts.

An individual must follow and understand not only another's speech, gestures, facial expressions, and body language, but also the context, environment, and situation being referred to by the speaker. This requires that a person process and integrate a multitude of information almost simultaneously. This is very difficult and almost impossible for the child with autism and sensory dysfunction.

Children and adults with sensory integration dysfunction experience difficulties in some or all areas of communication. Their inability to comprehend (receptive language) can be a problem, as well as their inability to express themselves verbally and nonverbally.

Accurate receptive language involves processing what a person hears when trying to understand another person. For example, a child that is hyper-responsive to sound may tune out a speaker. If he is mono-channeled and can only process one sense at a time, then listening to the teacher in a classroom setting may be impossible because of distracting movement in the room—other students too close to him, students touching him periodically, etc. An adult with mild auditory issues told a speech therapist that in a noisy setting he would resort to lip reading. Some individuals, when under stress or tired or ill, lose their ability to process what they hear. For individuals with sensory integration dysfunction, one can only imagine the amount of information that is never captured due to difficulty in processing.

Expressive language requires the ability to mechanically produce numerous sounds and sound combinations, know the meaning of countless words, and know the rules of how these words go together (grammar) to form negatives, questions, and complex sentences. Proficient communicators also communicate nonverbally by using body language, facial expressions, and culturally accepted signs (such as waving and pointing) to convey information. Typically when we refer to language, we mean that which is verbal. However, sign language is also a recognized language. It fulfills these requirements and has its own vocabulary and rules for putting words together in a systematic way.

Children with ASD and sensory integration dysfunction frequently exhibit echolalic speech. They repeat what is said. Even though this is a typical stage of speech development that children go through as they learn to speak, echolalic speech often remains well after it is chronologically appropriate for the child with autism. Echolalic behaviors range from the repetition of sounds to words, phrases, or entire scripts previously heard. For some individuals, echolalic speech remains the primary source of communication.

In his work, *Communication and Language Issues in Autism and Pervasive Developmental Disabilities: A Transactional Perspective,* Dr. Barry Prizant delineates a hierarchy of echolalic behavior. Dr. Prizant says that a child may initially repeat, without comprehension, what he has heard immediately after a model. This may be followed by the child repeating, with understanding, either immediately after or in a delayed fashion. For example, one can ask a child "Do you want juice?" and the child's response is "Do you want juice?" Mitigated echolalia occurs when the child is able to alter and personalize what has been modeled. For example, you may ask a child "Do you want juice?" and he responds "I want juice."

An individual may produce stereotypic vocalizations/verbalizations— speech that is repeated over and over. These utterances can consist of repetition of sounds, words, phrases, and even longer scripts, such as jingles, commercials, and videos. A person may do this for a variety of reasons. Individuals may use utterances to calm themselves when stressed, to self-prompt when they execute an activity, or to block out painful stimuli.

The study of language includes the functional aspects of communication: when, how, and why. Whom do we tell when we are not feeling well— a stranger on the street, a parent, or the doctor? How do we know when we are beginning to bore the listener with our conversation? The social aspect of language remains one of the most difficult areas for individuals with sensory integration dysfunction to master because they must be able to process even the subtlest of cues. At the most severe end of the spectrum, some individuals with autism do not know that speech is used for communication.

Inappropriate pitch and intonation patterns may occur in many children. For some children, perhaps as the result of faulty auditory processing, speech may sound very robotic and monotone. For others, speech may exhibit a highly exaggerated intonation pattern similar to the ones used in commercials or cartoons. This may be the result of speech that is echolalic in nature, and the child is repeating "exactly" as it was heard.

Accurate body awareness, and in turn, motor planning or praxis, impacts communication on many levels. From a gross motor perspective, how can a child learn to wave when he lacks body awareness and may not even know that he has an arm?

Specific oral issues can range from mild to severe. The integration of the tactile and the proprioceptive senses is necessary for an individual to be able to adequately plan and execute the various sounds needed for speech. The speed with which sounds are produced, the pressure of the lips, and the appropriate placement of the tongue and lips are only some of the variables that are affected when these senses are not functioning optimally.

In summary, sensory integration deficits, such as poor body/oral awareness, attention difficulties, and high levels of arousal, directly impact an individual's ability to communicate. At the most basic level, one must have good self- and body-awareness in order to use his body for communication.

Ryan   *Ryan, a two-year-old nonverbal child, uses position to express a limited number of needs. He stands by the refrigerator to let his mother know that he wants something to eat and stands by the front door to indicate he would like to go for a walk. He does not point for wanted items, clap hands to convey enjoyment, or wave.*

The therapist encouraged Ryan to wave good-bye by imitation, as it naturally occurred at the end of each session. Despite many weeks of modeling a wave, Ryan did not catch on. The speech therapist tried using physical prompts by holding his arm firmly and waving, providing increased proprioceptive feedback. Immediately, Ryan looked at his arm as if he were aware of it for the first time.

Chapter Two

Sensory Processing Difficulties

An overview of each sensory system, including associated difficulties and behaviors, provides essential information needed prior to intervention planning. At times, the observable behaviors may be the individual's only means of communication.

Vestibular System

- Provides the unconscious information from the inner ear about one's equilibrium (state of balance) and head and body movements away from, and to, the center of gravity.

- Provides a sense of security and ties us to the ground.

- Sends information to all parts of the brain.

- Receives input from body movement and movement in the environment.

The vestibular system facilitates a sustained calm, alert, attentional state. It can be called the "unifying system" because it provides the foundation for the effective functioning of the other systems. The vestibular system and auditory system are closely related, and difficulties in these areas can impact speech and language development. Attention to what is being said is needed for language comprehension and speech to develop. The vestibular system helps the brain organize and process what is being said, facilitating the development of language comprehension and speech. Slow, linear movement is calming; fast movement is stimulating/arousing.

Individuals who have difficulty with vestibular input may underregister sensory input, overregister sensory input, or display evidence of both. Behavioral manifestations of vestibular underregistration include seeking increased movement (e.g., pacing, spurts of running, rocking) or an entire lack of awareness of the vestibular input.

Underregistration of vestibular input also impacts posture, which often results in "floppy" or low tone. Observable behaviors include leaning on objects such as walls for support, slumping at a table, or using arms for support during transitional movements (such as rising from a chair or the floor). A person expends much energy to compensate for decreased tone and lack of body support.

The vestibular system facilitates coordination of eye and neck muscles to adjust for head movements. Decreased registration of vestibular input impacts the coordination of eye, head, and body movements. This coordination is necessary to develop refined motor skills, such as writing or catching a ball.

Individuals who have low registration of vestibular input often crave movement in order to achieve an optimal level of arousal. As mentioned previously, stereotypic seeking behaviors include rocking, impulsive running, spinning, and pacing. Movement may also be due to difficulties with balance reactions, such as maintaining sitting posture on a classroom chair.

Overregistration of vestibular input is often referred to as gravitational insecurity, or fear of movement. These individuals often have an exaggerated fear of falling and exhibit difficulty walking from one surface to another. A pause when going from grass to concrete or from a carpeted area to one with tiles is a clue. Gait may be affected: Walking with a shuffling gait allows the individual to keep both feet on the ground.

These individuals feel most comfortable with as little head movement as possible. They may keep their necks and heads rigid during tasks such as eating. Avoiding tasks that require looking down and up, such as copying from a board or playing cards, is common. These individuals may be taxed if we put them in a position that requires a lot of head movement.

In both of these cases of vestibular difficulties, the individual tends to manipulate the environment. One individual finds it more comfortable not to move, and the other is moving like crazy and not getting much out of it.

Postural insecurity is another term often used to describe fear of movement. There is a distinction between gravitational insecurity and postural insecurity. The individual with postural insecurity is fearful of movement because she lacks her own external supports—often due to neuromuscular issues such as cerebral palsy. However, once positioned correctly and provided with the needed support, the individual tolerates and may even enjoy movement. The individual with gravitational insecurity, on the other hand, has the neuromuscular supports and yet does not tolerate movement.

Saul   *At first glance, Saul, a seven-year-old with a diagnosis of autism, appeared to demonstrate motor skills appropriate for his age. He could walk on a balance beam, climb, and jump like any child his age. Further observation revealed Saul's slightly low tone.*

He exhibited a slumped posture and preferred sitting on the floor to sitting on a chair. Saul "crashed" or collapsed onto the floor during transitions. He required his arms for support when rising from the floor. He lacked the ability to maintain a workable sitting posture without keeping one hand on the floor for support, which in turn limited his bilateral hand skills. Functionally, Saul used an enormous amount of energy for simple tasks. He exhibited underregistration of vestibular input.

Alex   *Alex, a nine-year-old boy with a diagnosis of autism, was referred to occupational therapy for a handwriting problem. His teacher said that Alex was able to write dictated spelling words accurately when performing these tasks at the blackboard. However, these skills were lost when Alex had to spell the words and look at the teacher while seated at his desk. Additionally, the teacher reported that when she spoke to the class from her desk, Alex was able to attend for most of the discussion. However, when she lectured while moving about the classroom, his attention was replaced with self-stimulating behavior (hand flapping). It was evident that Alex overregistered vestibular input.*

Vestibular input is received not only from oneself but also from environmental movement—such as the movement of others. When observing his teacher moving about, Alex used hand flapping to tune out the uncomfortable sensory input.

Proprioceptive System

- Provides unconscious information from muscles and joints.

- Gives information about movement and changes of position in space and the pressure and stretch of muscles and joints.

- Provides body scheme/awareness.

Proprioception is our "internal eyes." It is the sense that provides body scheme, which in turn allows for accurate motor planning. Accurate motor planning involves

Ideation: The conceptualizing of an idea or concept.

Planning: The ability to internally organize how to move, know the sequence of actions and timing needed, and visualize the end result.

Visualizing or knowing what the end result of an action will be is known as "feed forward."

Execution: The ability to perform the purposeful action within one's environment. Proprioceptive input also provides the needed feedback during (and following) an action.

One receives proprioceptive information when muscles contract and stretch and joints bend. This sense facilitates smooth movements by providing information about where one's body begins and ends and about one's location in relation to the environment without constant visual cuing. Examples of proprioceptive tasks performed without visual monitoring include gesturing, pointing, and writing.

When writing, proprioception provides a sense of the pressure applied to the pencil point so that one does not press too hard or too lightly. Proprioceptive input during writing also enables the hand to guide the pencil's movements along the paper and provides feedback from the hand as to where it is in space. When people write, they look at what they are writing; they do not visually monitor their hand and arm movements. Writing difficulties can include breaking of pencil points and difficulty in forming letters and words.

Gross, fine, and oral motor skills are impacted by proprioceptive difficulties. The individual with proprioceptive issues may appear clumsy and bump into things. She may lack the skills to accurately judge the distance between herself and a wall and catch her shoulder in a doorway or going around a corner. One may observe a child who has difficulty positioning herself squarely on furniture, which in turn affects tabletop tasks as she attempts to balance herself.

Poor processing of proprioception often limits an individual's repertoire of motor skills, hindering effective interaction with the environment. Issues with self-help skills such as dressing may occur. Clothing management may be difficult because accurate body awareness is necessary to arrange clothing appropriately.

Oral motor difficulties may occur, which can impact speech and/or feeding. The individual who does not know where to place her tongue in her mouth will have difficulty forming sounds and words. Inaccurate tongue movements during feeding may result in a poorly formed food bolus and cause choking.

Proprioception is stimulated through deep pressure touch and by heavy work patterns such as pushing, pulling, or carrying. Proprioceptive input is calming; therefore, in an effort to calm themselves, individuals may engage in proprioceptive seeking behaviors, such as rubbing or banging their hands together, pushing into others and objects, stuffing food, mouthing nonedibles, and grinding teeth.

Tactile System

The tactile system is the sense of touch: There are tactile receptors on the skin and inside the mouth that respond to all types of touch. The receptors allow accurate interpretation of light touch, pain, temperature, and pressure. Integration of the tactile system, along with the vestibular and proprioceptive systems, allows accurate speech articulation. Light touch is alerting; firm or pressure touch is calming.

The tactile system requires constant stimulation to keep oneself organized and functioning. Tactile input is ongoing, either through actively touching or being passively touched. There are two types of tactile systems: One is responsible for exploration, learning, and discrimination, and the other is responsible for defense. The defense system protects us from dangerous touch such as sharp objects or temperature extremes. Individuals who do not process tactile information effectively also may not have accurate awareness of temperature and pain.

Overregistration of tactile input, often referred to as tactile defensiveness, occurs when nonthreatening touch is perceived as threatening. When one overregisters tactile input, the defensive system "kicks in" rather than the system used to explore and discriminate. One may seek her space and appear fearful or angry when approached. When she is in close proximity to others, she may hit or push in an effort to increase her personal space.

Resistance to self-help skills is common. Grooming tasks such as brushing the teeth, washing the face, and brushing the hair can all be painful experiences for the individual who is overregistering tactile input. There may be discomfort with clothing of certain fabrics, new clothing, and seams or labels. Clothing touching one's body may cause fidgeting and 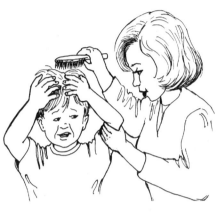 discomfort when sitting in a place too long. As a child becomes an adolescent, undergarments such as bras can be an issue. When touched, the individual may rub or scratch that body part. A preoccupation with cleanliness can occur.

The mouth may be sensitive, and independent feeding skills can be delayed. Going from a liquid to a solid diet could be difficult. The individual may refuse to use certain utensils or try new foods due to texture or temperature issues.

Avoidance of tasks may delay motor skill development. For example, an individual may not want to hold a pencil or have her hand rub on the paper when writing. She may avoid gross motor activities that involve contact, such as kicking or catching a ball. Sensitivity to extreme temperature or weather may cause agitation or fear, hindering one's desire to go outside. Feet may be sensitive and impact one's gait. In an effort to avoid tactile input, a person may walk on tiptoes. Over time, this can cause orthopedic issues such as shortening of the heel cords.

Cal   *Cal, a four-year-old boy, was referred for an occupational therapy evaluation due to delays with fine motor skills. Age-appropriate manipulative skills, such as the ability to copy simple strokes or snip paper, were not emerging. During the evaluation, it became obvious that due to tactile sensitivity, Cal avoided these tasks, as well as others that required tactile exploration. A program to address his tactile defensiveness included activities that provided proprioceptive input to override his heightened tactile system and vestibular input (such as slow swinging) to facilitate a calmer level of arousal. Subsequently, as Cal's tactile defensiveness decreased, the therapist observed greater exploration of manipulative tasks. Cal's fine motor skill deficits resolved. Once able to hold the pencil without the painful effects of overregistration of tactile input, Cal was not only able to imitate simple strokes but was also able to write his name and that of his classmates independently!*

An individual who underregisters tactile input may display either a decreased awareness of, or a tremendous need for, tactile input. She may have a high tolerance for pain, unwittingly injuring herself. The individual may seek tactile stimulation through mouthing objects or placing hands in the mouth. The individual may constantly rub or touch objects or people (or touch herself inappropriately). Poor tactile feedback may cause delayed, decreased, or sometimes a complete lack of response to tactile input.

Jeff   *Jeff, an eighteen-year-old with autism, craved touch. He manipulated objects by rubbing them until his fingers bled. Jeff was unaware of pain and was known to place his hands on a hot burner.*

Accurate tactile feedback from the articulators (lips, tongue, and cheeks) allows for the production of clear speech. Oral feedback that is inaccurate hinders one's perception of the location, degree of pressure, and speed with which articulators function within the mouth, resulting in poorly produced speech.

Auditory System

The auditory system is the hearing sense that allows accurate interpretation of speech and environmental sounds. It is closely associated with the vestibular system. Soft voices are calming; loud noises are alerting.

Normal hearing acuity does not guarantee speech. A person must be able to attend, process, remember, and interpret sounds. The vestibular system is housed within the inner ear, and it is the integration of the auditory and vestibular systems that is needed for accurate processing of auditory information. In other words, it is understanding what is being said and ultimately learning to speak. Stimulation of the vestibular system directly impacts the auditory system and language. It is not uncommon to note an increase of vocalizations when the vestibular system is stimulated through swinging and rocking.

Under- or overregistration of auditory input can impact a person's functioning in many ways. In *Asperger's Syndrome*, Dr. Tony Attwood (1998) describes noises that some people feel as intense. These include sudden, unexpected noises such as a dog barking or a phone ringing; high pitched, continuous noises like small electrical appliances; and confusing, complex sounds such as a noisy shopping center.

"Superhearing" refers to individuals who are unable to filter out extraneous noises such as a refrigerator running, a clock ticking, or the sound of students walking in a hallway. Loud places like lunchrooms, echoing rooms, crowded hallways, and shopping malls may cause an increase in one's level of arousal. The sound of wind or rain may make the outdoors unbearable.

Wes   *Wes was a very social young man who enjoyed people and loved talking on the phone. However, getting him to leave the house was a constant chore. The wind was so painful for Wes that he needed to wear a hooded sweater, even in warm weather, to protect himself from the sounds of even the lightest breeze.*

Self-care skills, such as washing one's ears or getting haircuts, may pose problems. The sound of running water can cause discomfort and result in toilet training delays or other bathroom issues. When auditory input becomes too intense, the individual may use her own voice to tune out the painful input. However, there can be a fine line between the behavioral manifestations of over- and underregistration of auditory input. Vocalizations can also be due to seeking auditory input or as a way to provide tactile stimulation in the mouth.

Individuals may also cover their ears, grimace from sounds, or tune out all sounds to the point that they appear to be deaf. Appearing as if one is deaf may be the result of underregistration of input, as well as tuning out the input due to the perceived intensity (overregistration).

Pamela II   Here are two e-mails from Tammy G. regarding her daughter Pamela's eating difficulties:

> *I had an interesting cyber conversation with a very high-functioning gentleman with autism. I asked him if he had any idea why Pamela hates to use utensils. He suggested that it might be the noise of scraping silverware against a glass dish. So we switched to plastic. He also suggested I explain why we use utensils as he finds it hard to accept things that seem to have no purpose. I did. I told Pamela she is a big girl now, and if she eats like a baby, people won't know how smart she is. It may be my imagination, but I did not have to spend the whole meal correcting her. We'll see what develops over the next few days!*

And now...   *Pamela no longer resists using utensils. She even puts a spoon in one hand and a fork in the other. She never seemed to "get" that* *before, and she started doing this on her own because the clanging noise is not there. (Pamela now uses all utensils.)*

When learning a new task, the interventionist needs to decrease other distractions. Once the task is learned, reintroduce environmental stressors because they are easier to tolerate without the demands of learning a new task.

Visual System

Vision is the process that enables a person to make sense of what is seen. Minimal background stimulus is calming. Excessive background stimulus is arousing.

Integration of visual stimuli with other sensory input is necessary for an accurate understanding of what one sees. Poor modulation of visual stimuli may result in "super vision" due to an inability to block out or filter unnecessary stimuli. Increased agitation may occur in environments with multiple stimuli.

Individuals may seek visual input through self-stimulating behaviors such as waving their hands in front of their eyes. Individuals may spend long periods of time staring into the sunlight, which can create a "break" from environmental stressors, but the behavior has the potential to cause damage to the eyes. Although these individuals possess accurate visual acuity, at times they may act as if they cannot see or may even look through people.

Olfactory System

Olfactory receptors located in the nose allow for the sense of smell. Smell and taste are closely related. Soft and mild odors like vanilla are often calming; however, all odors have the potential to be alerting.

A person who demonstrates difficulties with the olfactory system may find any environment overpowering. Observable behaviors may include obsessive smelling or extreme aversive reactions to substances.

Bill   *Incense, used during a church service, caused Bill to be physically ill and vomit.*

Oral/Feeding Difficulties

Robert   *Robert, a two-year-old boy, would not eat his favorite bread if it was "torn." Leonard, a sixteen-year-old, would stuff an excessive amount of food in his mouth. Cory, age one, held his lips in a tight pucker for 20 minutes following any feeding interventions. One four-year-old's diet consisted of a limited assortment of foods that could only be eaten at room temperature. All of these feeding difficulties were due to sensory integration dysfunction.*

Feeding issues related to sensory integration dysfunction are mainly issues of quality rather than neuromuscular or structural difficulties that may interfere with swallowing or the mechanics of eating. The complexities of the sensory issues have the potential to cause significant health issues and render this problem area one of the most difficult to work with.

In order to simplify the task of addressing this issue, this section is divided by sensory system. Two types of oral sensory dysfunction, "hyper" (overregistration or defensiveness) and "hypo" (underregistration), are noted with the understanding that there can be numerous other variables that may impact feeding.

Individuals with sensory integration-based feeding difficulties often deal with numerous other issues. The sensory input within the oral mechanism and characteristics of the food directly impact them. External environmental events and internal vestibular and proprioceptive issues indirectly impact the individuals. The therapists must assess and address all of these during feeding treatment. As with other sensory integration issues, oral motor problems can range from mild to severe.

Gustatory/Taste Disturbances

The following is a sampling of possible behaviors caused by gustatory/taste disturbances. The letters in parentheses indicate whether the difficulty is typically the result of over- (O) or under- (U) registration.

The individual reacts to the taste of certain foods.

- Eats only select items (O)

- Eats only strong-tasting or bland-tasting food (O)

- Does not distinguish foods (U)

- Puts non-food items in mouth: Pica (U)

Proprioceptive/Tactile Disturbances

The individual reacts to the feel of a substance and to the pressure within the oral cavity.

- Eats only soft foods (O)

- Does not chew (O)

- Too easily elicits gag reflex (O)

- Avoids certain textures (e.g., grainy) (O)

- Avoids finger feeding (O)

- Is sensitive to food temperature (O)

- Stuffs food (U) (Stuffing of food is normal to age 18 months.)

- Grinds teeth (U)

- Has hands always in mouth (U)

- Seeks only crunchy or chewy foods (U)

- Has a preoccupation with playing with food (U)

Infants may exhibit poor sucking and/or rooting abilities. They may fall asleep as soon as hunger pains subside, following only a short period of sucking. Difficulty in transitioning to table food can occur in early childhood.

Auditory/Hearing Disturbances

- Resists eating due to sound produced while chewing (O)

Olfactory/Smell Disturbances

- Overreacts to nonnoxious smells (e.g., gagging) (O)

- Smells food prior to eating (U)

Visual Disturbances

- Insists on sameness (e.g., color, shape)

Chapter Three

Sensory-Based Behaviors

Sensory Defensiveness

When I was an infant, my senses didn't work right and my response to light, and sound, and touch, were not just meaningless but too acute. I could not only not understand the world, but I also could not stand it.

Donna Williams,
Autism: An Inside Out Approach, 1996

People with sensory integration difficulties frequently show signs of sensory defensiveness and react negatively or with anxiety to sensory input that is generally considered harmless or nonirritating to other people. Individuals who overregister sensory information experience sensory defensiveness.

Sensory defensiveness occurs in one or several sensory systems. It is a painful and uncomfortable experience and can impact the ability to attend and participate in life tasks. An individual can perceive voices as aversive—comparable to the sound of nails on a blackboard. A simple touch on the hand may feel like hot coals. Even the memory of an aversive experience can trigger physical distress.

Peter   *Peter, a two-year-old with severe tactile defensiveness, would physically gag and cry at the sight of a can of Funny Color Foam, a soap for children, because of the bad memory of previously touching it.*

The severity of sensory defensiveness ranges from mild to severe. The individuals with a mild impairment may be considered "picky" because they avoid unpleasant experiences. When confronted with an aversive situation, they deal with it, but they use an increased amount of energy.

Several areas of life, such as self-care tasks or social interactions, can be affected for those with moderate sensory defensiveness. For those individuals, addressing and treating their sensory defensiveness enables them to participate in life experiences.

Severe sensory defensiveness affects all aspects of life. These individuals typically have other diagnoses, ranging from autism to tuberous sclerosis, in addition to sensory integration dysfunction. Appendix A includes additional information about a variety of conditions that may involve severe sensory defensiveness.

Treatment of sensory defensiveness facilitates a more appropriate level of arousal and allows increased exploration of the environment. For those severely affected, reduction of sensory defensiveness allows the therapist to treat other areas of concern, such as communication, motor skills, socialization, and academics, in order to enhance the quality of life.

Self-Abusive and Self-Stimulating Behaviors

Self-abusive behavior—the attempt to injure oneself—is almost always in response to stress. Noise, visual stimuli, or the movement of others in the environment all may be too much for a person with sensory defensiveness. The interventionists may consider the environment appropriate, but individuals with sensory processing difficulties may not be able to tolerate it.

Engaging in self-abusive behavior allows for blocking out the painful environmental input. Less frequently, particularly if the behavior is new, self-abusive behavior may indicate illness. Head banging can be an indication of an earache, toothache, or headache. One report describes an individual with autism who banged his head to "get the pain out."

Repetitive, stereotypic, self-stimulating behaviors may also be the result of sensory defensiveness in an attempt to calm and gain relief from the painful stress of the stimuli. Additionally, poor motor planning skills limit many of these individuals' repertoire of movement. One can also observe self-stimulating behavior when the individual is not engaged in purposeful activity. This can be likened to "finger tapping" or "doodling." Dysfunctional, self-stimulating behaviors, often evident when an individual is not engaged, frequently diminish when the individual is engaged in a motivating task.

Edward *Edward, an eleven-year-old boy with autism, presented numerous self-stimulating, ritualistic behaviors. Dropping plastic bottles off counters, smearing gel-type substances such as liquid detergent on his body, and hand flapping were only some of his frequently observed behaviors. When Edward was engaged in play on the trampoline with his brother, he was entirely different. He was attentive, followed cues, and stopped self-stimulatory behaviors.*

Prompt Dependency

Children with sensory integration difficulties who exhibit poor body awareness are frequently unable to independently complete motor tasks. They easily become dependent on others to help with task completion. When attempting to teach a skill, therapists frequently use physical prompts or passive movement, such as hand-over-hand assistance, to "take one through" the motor action. However, taking one through a motor action rather than encouraging independent performance hinders the development of coordinated actions and active movement. This results in prompt dependency, or reliance on an external cue (e.g., a therapist), in order to complete a task.

Accurate processing of visual and proprioceptive information (internal and external "eyes") facilitates the development of coordinated movements or motor planning. Active, independent movement is critical for integrating these two senses and can only be achieved by decreasing physical prompts or passive movement. Use physical prompts as infrequently as possible. Always allow for the opportunity of even partial independent performance.

When possible, change the position of the provided physical support from direct control to indirect control. For example, during feeding, when the child becomes more adept at this skill, move physical support from the child's hand (direct control) to his wrist and then eventually gently guide at the elbow (indirect control).

Gradually moving from a firm, constant touch for support to a more intermittent touch with less pressure is another way to reduce prompt dependency and facilitate independence. Use caution with soft touch if the child has tactile sensitivity. Guidance through a motor action by the interventionist placing his or her hands near the child (but not touching the child) can provide a gentle physical "barrier" and allow for "a no-hands approach."

Reverse chaining (allowing the individual to complete the last part of a task) while gradually expanding the motor demand is one way to decrease assistance and foster independence. For example, when hand-over-hand assistance is initially needed for self-feeding, remove support when the spoon is just about to reach the child's lips.

Children can also become verbally prompt dependent (i.e., a child depends on a verbal cue to speak or to complete a motor action). For example, Matthew only greets and says "Hi" when given the directive "Say 'Hi,' Matthew." Matthew will only wave good-bye when prompted with the verbal directive "Wave 'bye-bye.'"

When teaching a child a new skill, whether it be motor, verbal, or social, the first step is to ensure (as much as possible) that the skill is at the child's instructional level. For example, one cannot expect a child to learn to use complete sentences when he is just beginning to use single words, just as a child cannot be expected to run if he is just learning to walk.

While the interventionist must initially provide as much support as necessary in order to successfully accomplish the task, once the child has demonstrated the ability to produce the skill, provide practice opportunities as often as possible with as little support as possible. A good rule of thumb is to help as much as necessary—but no more.

For verbal tasks, the hierarchy of more-to-less support generally begins with full modeling. For example, the speech therapist may begin by saying the word(s) for the child to repeat (e.g., "puppy") with a visual such as the object itself or a picture. The therapist then progresses to saying the beginning part of the word. Eventually, the therapist directs the child to a visual prompt of a "puppy" when soliciting production of the word. Posting the picture and the word "puppy" in the child's environment provides a way for him to verbalize independently.

Billy   *Billy, a seven-year-old boy with significant physical and cognitive delays, had no functional language. He responded to yes/no questions by nodding his head. When Billy was asked a question that he wanted to answer "Yes," he would take his own hand and gently push his head in an up-and-down movement. This suggests that this motor action may have been taught with extensive physical prompts, which then became part of this routine. Billy was prompt dependent; pushing his own head forward had become part of nodding.*

Peter   *Peter, a two-year-old boy who possibly had autism, did not use his hands as developmentally appropriate for his age in play or to explore objects. For example, he held items in his hands without manipulating or exploring them.*

Peter was interested in a musical form board that had several cutout shapes such as a circle, square, triangle, diamond, etc. When all the pieces are in the correct place, the form board plays music as a reinforcer.

Initially, Peter wanted to push the form piece into the board and elicit the desired sound; however, he was unable to figure out how to use his hands for this task. He finally accomplished this task by pushing the piece into the puzzle with his nose. Peter was only able to complete motor tasks with his hands when provided full physical assistance by the interventionist. She firmly took Peter's hand and moved it through the complete motor action. Full physical assistance was gradually decreased, and games were provided that increased proprioceptive input, such as holding Peter's hands and pulling and pushing during "Row, Row, Row Your Boat." Within a short time, Peter became more aware of his body and attempted to use his hands for placement of the shapes into the board.

Hierarchy of Prompts at a Glance

Motor Prompts

Full hand-over-hand assistance

Direct to indirect assistance

Constant touch to intermittent touch with decreasing pressure

Reverse chaining

No "hands-on" physical guidance

Verbal Prompts

Modeling word(s) with visual

Partial modeling with visual

Cue with visual

Visual in environment

Chapter Four

Approach to Intervention

Over the years, we have identified a few basic principles that guide our approach to treatment. Understanding that working with individuals with sensory integration disorders is as much an art as it is a science drives our therapy approach.

"Science" provides ongoing information about the disorders that enables occupational therapists (OTs), speech-language pathologists (SLPs), and other interventionists to work from a sound knowledge base.

"Art" is created when interventionists read and respond effectively to subtle cues and unconventional behaviors. Knowing when to continue with a task, when to take a break, or when to change the format or presentation of information are all examples of the "art" of treatment.

For individuals with sensory integration dysfunction, these issues must be addressed because they will affect focus, ongoing attention, and learning. The treatment approach should be sensory-based, yet eclectic. Sensory integration strategies imbedded throughout the day, as needed, can easily work with other programs in which an individual may be participating.

Activities are "individual-directed and therapist-controlled." The person's interests and needs drive the tasks. However, OTs, SLPs, and other interventionists set the parameters in order to enhance learning.

Use the child's strengths and interests to motivate her. This will facilitate engagement, increase participation, and enhance overall quality of learning. A child who is preoccupied with letters may participate in a cutting task if letters are the objects to be cut. The individual who

is preoccupied with stereotypic, repetitive dropping of plastic objects may participate in bowling if plastic bottles are used for the task.

Learning requires active participation. Decreasing physical and verbal prompts is essential for learning because a person can easily become dependent on prompts for task completion. The integration of visual and proprioceptive input requires active movement to develop. Taking an individual through an activity with total hand-over-hand assistance inhibits motor learning.

Processing and executing tasks frequently require increased time. Interventionists should provide sufficient time for smooth transitions.

Communication among all those participating in a child's education is critical. Teaming should occur across all settings, from home to school to work, etc. Parents, educators, physicians, administrators, and therapists must all come together for optimal programming and an integrated, consistent approach to learning.

Ongoing assessment and continuous observation of behaviors and responses to input are necessary so that the appropriate intervention can take place.

Therapeutic Approach

• Combine Art and Science

• Be Sensory-Based, Yet Eclectic

• Keep It Individual-Directed, Therapist-Controlled

• Teach to Strengths

• Provide Motivation

• Encourage Active Participation

• Provide Time

• Work as a Team

• Blend Therapies and Disciplines

• Conduct Ongoing Assessments

Treatment Cycle

In order for learning to take place, one must be able to attend and maintain attention. Look at intervention as a treatment cycle that can be used throughout the day to enhance overall functioning.

- Provide sensory integration strategies to modulate an individual's level of arousal and enhance her ability to attend and prepare for learning.

- Provide a balance between calming activities and challenging tasks that require participation and response. Over time, task demands tend to raise an individual's level of arousal.

- Monitor the individual's level of arousal while she performs tasks.

- If arousal level is elevated, decrease demands and once again provide sensory integration strategies.

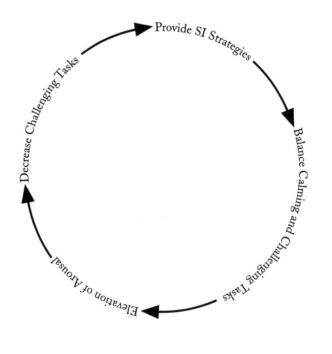

Teaming

Everybody brings something to the party!

Linus Van Pelt

The cooperative effort of sharing ideas, expertise, and work leads to the formation of a team. Teaming occurs at different levels, depending on the needs being addressed. Cotreatment and consultation are vehicles for ongoing communication among disciplines, with active involvement of parents and caretakers being essential in this therapeutic process. Teaming and the blending of therapies facilitate completion of a comprehensive intervention plan for the home, classroom, or residential setting.

Although the concept of teaming is not unique, experience demonstrates that effective teaming is an ongoing and always evolving process, leading to the continuous development of new techniques and strategies. Teaming facilitates communication and results in treating the individual with a holistic approach rather than a segmented one.

Team members are aware of all areas of development and their relationship to the individual's specific needs, thus facilitating functional skill development as it naturally occurs. For example, the occupational therapist becomes more aware of the communicative intent of some motor actions. The speech therapist works on communication skills while being aware of how sensory processing issues will impact a child's level of arousal. The result of working together is synergistic, as several "heads together" often elicit more creative interventions.

Working with individuals with sensory integration issues is often a long and arduous task because many areas of development are impacted. Sharing this responsibility among team members allows for problem solving and the identification of solutions to sometimes difficult issues.

At times, more hands are needed. For example, one team member may engage the child, while the member of another discipline may impact her posture. Over time, teaming becomes transdisciplinary as different disciplines assume each other's roles as needed. This allows for seizing numerous teachable moments, opportunities that often come unexpectedly! All parties gain new and necessary tools to facilitate overall development in those people with sensory integration issues.

Benefits of Teaming

- Provides a Holistic Approach

- Creates Synergy

- Shares Responsibility

- Provides More Hands

- Enhances Transdisciplinary Intervention

- Facilitates Seizing the Moment

- Fosters Professional Growth

Teaming with Jon & Sammi

Public Law 94-142 opened the doors for therapeutic services for infants and toddlers. Jon and Sammi were two youngsters who were initially served by the speech therapist. Sammi, a two-year-old, was a premature baby with residual visual impairments. Jon, also age two, had a diagnosis of tuberous sclerosis.

In both cases, these children resisted engagement—obtaining and maintaining their attention was next to impossible. Jon spent most of his time running around the room and placing everything in his mouth. Sammi would stiffen when held. When not engaged, she would spend extended periods of time looking at the light through the window blinds or looking, at a very close distance, at the lights on various toys. Sammi also had significant feeding issues. She avoided going from one food texture to another, eating only a few, selected items. Initial therapy with both children was inadequate.

Adding an occupational therapist provided sensory integration techniques and strategies. This assisted in preparing these children for learning. The children's needs were jointly addressed from a sensory and communicative perspective. As a team, the OT and SLP were better able to impact treatment.

Armond   *Armond, a handsome boy diagnosed with autism, began receiving speech therapy when he was about five. At the time, he attended a noncategorical preschool classroom. He participated in speech therapy with a group of three or four other students. Twice a week, the group would walk across a playground to the trailer that housed the therapy room. On the walk back, Armond frequently would run away from the group. The speech therapist was faced with a dilemma. Should she run after him and leave the group or let him go and hope that he would arrive at his classroom promptly?*

After learning about the sensory issues that affect many individuals with autism, the therapist thought that these group therapy sessions must have been terribly taxing on Armond. He had to sit close to other students and experience a noisy, visually busy environment.

Armond is now an adult. A few years ago, a therapist asked if he recalled running away from the group; he responded that he did. Then came the big question: "Why?" The therapist expected him to respond that it was because of stress and anxiety due to an overload of sensory experiences. Armond instead simply stated, "It was so much fun."

Armond's story serves as a reminder that as we assess individuals for sensory integration dysfunction, we must keep matters in perspective. Individuals exhibit behaviors for a variety of reasons: to get attention, obtain something, or avoid something. Other reasons may include boredom, difficulty with sensory experiences, and, of course, because "it was so much fun."

Chapter Five

Assessment

An initial evaluation serves as an introduction to an individual's overall development and function, as well as his strengths and needs. This information lays the groundwork for an effective prescriptive plan of action.

When working with individuals with sensory and communication problems, direct hands-on testing and standardized testing are often difficult or impossible to secure. The continuous transitions from task to task, time factors, and at times, difficulty with understanding the task itself, frequently result in incomplete and inaccurate information. Strategies such as direct observation, interviews with significant others, communication samples, and when possible, videos of the individual in his natural environment complement standardized testing and result in a more reliable profile.

Observations across settings allow for enhanced accuracy in identifying abilities and difficulties. Ensure that observed behaviors are typical and not due to fatigue, hunger, medication changes, or undiagnosed illness. Dental issues, stomach problems, and earaches can all produce behavioral changes.

Some conditions, including those on the autism spectrum, are behaviorally defined—there are no medical tests that can diagnose these conditions. Ideally, medical and school personnel use developmental screening instruments as a first step when there are possible concerns. Filipek et al. (1999) provides specific practice parameters for the screening, evaluation, and diagnosis of individuals within the autism spectrum. Medical information and hearing and vision screenings are necessary.

An interdisciplinary team of specialists is the ideal choice when diagnosing these conditions. The team may include medical specialists, a psychologist, an educational diagnostician, an occupational therapist, a speech-language pathologist, a physical therapist, a social worker, an audiologist, and other professionals as needed. Parents play a critical role in the diagnostic process. Research findings indicate that parental concerns about a child's development are generally correct.

A strong indicator of high risk for autism is the lack of joint attention—a skill observed in children before age one. Joint attention is a group of behaviors that includes pointing, seeking eye contact, following direction of another person's gaze, and vocalizing or verbalizing to share or show interest. Other critical indicators of possible autism include lack of babbling or gesturing (waving, pointing) by twelve months, no single words by sixteen months, lack of two-word spontaneous phrases (not echolalic) by twenty-four months, or loss of language or social skills at any age.

Communication

Speech-language pathologists are the primary therapists responsible for the assessment and evaluation of communication. With younger children, initial concerns typically revolve around lack of (or delays in) speech. A thorough assessment is necessary, whether the individual is speaking or not. When possible, formal testing provides information about specific areas of speech and language. Formal instruments, however, are limited in their abilities to provide information about social communication skills.

SLPs should assess receptive language or comprehension with and without the use of contextual cues. Cues, such as an interventionist extending a hand when requesting an item, may provide the needed information rather than the understanding of the verbal directive. The assessment should include the individual's ability to comprehend words and the quantity and variety of the vocabulary used. SLPs also must examine the comprehension of simple-to-complex sentences, including use of negatives, questions, and conditional statements. When appropriate, the therapist should study the individual's ability to follow conversations and understand the more abstract elements of language (such as sarcasm and innuendoes).

An expressive evaluation should include how an individual communicates—from crying, to facial expressions, to gesturing, to using sounds, words, sentences, and complex utterances. Assess why the person communicates. Note if he is able to imitate, question, protest, obtain another's attention, greet, answer, and express feelings. Assessment of any alternative or augmentative system of communication, such as voice output devices, sign language, or picture exchange system, is essential.

A spontaneous language sample, with standardized tests, may provide an approximate profile of a child's receptive and expressive language. Popular instruments include vocabulary tests such as The Peabody Picture Vocabulary Test-3rd Edition, a norm-referenced, quickly administered, screening instrument for receptive vocabulary (ages 2.6 years through 90+) and The Expressive One-Word Picture Vocabulary Test-2000 Edition, a standardized assessment instrument that measures expressive vocabulary (ages 2 to 18 years).

There are several receptive and expressive language testing instruments available. The Preschool Language Scale-4 measures receptive and expressive language in children from birth through 6 years. The Receptive/Expressive Emergent Language Scale Revised-3 is a receptive and expressive language assessment instrument that also facilitates intervention planning for children ages birth to 3 years. The Sequenced Inventory of Communication Development - Revised assesses the communication skills of children who are developmentally functioning within the ages of 4 months through 4 years of age.

An examination of voice quality and articulation is an integral component of a thorough evaluation of verbal children. Some children with sensory integration difficulties exhibit oral motor planning issues that affect their ability to formulate and execute the complexity of oral movements required for speech. This is known as oral dyspraxia.

Sensory Motor

An occupational therapist with expertise in this area typically conducts the assessment of sensory integration/processing skills. Parent or caregiver reporting, clinical observations, and the use of commercial instruments provide a systematic way of gathering information and interpreting observed behaviors. The therapist may reach conclusions regarding the adequacy of the various systems, number of systems involved, degree of involvement, and impact the behavior has on the individual's function.

There are many formal instruments to assess sensory integration, for example the *Hawaii Early Learning Profile, Sensory Profile,* and *Sensory Integration Inventory-Revised for Individuals with Developmental Disabilities* .

The *Hawaii Early Learning Profile* is an assessment tool that breaks down motor, self-help, and behavior regulation for children between the ages of birth to 36 months. The *Sensory Profile* provides a standardized, judgment-based, caregiver questionnaire that is intended for children between 5-10 years, but it can be adapted for children 3-4 years. This tool measures a child's sensory processing abilities and their effects on his functional performance in daily life.

The *Sensory Integration Inventory-Revised for Individuals with Developmental Disabilities (SII-R)* is a screening instrument that assesses persons who might benefit from a sensory integration treatment approach. Although designed for adults, therapists can modify *SII-R* for children.

Specific behavioral observations should include, but not be limited to, investigating the individual's level of arousal across settings. Examine performance during play and leisure activities. Analyze the need for personal space, observe the reaction to others within the environment, and determine whether there are "avoiding or seeking behaviors."

Determine attention span and stamina by measuring how long a person remains on task. Once the individual is attending, note the ability to transition and shift attention. Assess ease of movement during physical transitions (such as moving from sitting to standing), overall muscle tone, and general posture. Observe motor planning skills as the individual navigates the environment.

Difficulties with sensory processing frequently lead to delays in motor output and development. Conversely, difficulties with motor output may hinder sensory development. As part of a comprehensive evaluation, occupational therapists routinely investigate not only sensory issues but also the individual's efficiency in the areas of fine motor, gross motor, and self-help skills.

Formal instruments that measure motor and self-help development provide useful information regarding current levels of performance and skills that are in need of further development. There are many formal evaluations available to assess motor and self-help skill levels.

Some formal instruments include The *Peabody Developmental Motor Scale-2nd Edition*, which measures gross and fine motor skills of children from birth to 83 months; the *Early Intervention Developmental Profile*; and the *Preschool Developmental Profile*. The last two are assessment-based programming instruments that provide developmental norms and milestones for children that function between the ages of birth to 35 months, and from 3 to 6 years, respectively.

The *Beery-Buktenica Developmental Test of Visual Motor Integration* assesses visual perception, motor coordination, and the integration of perception and motor coordination of individuals functioning in the age range of 2 to 19 years. The *School Function Assessment* helps identify a student's strengths and limitations while performing school-related functional tasks. This is a questionnaire that is completed by school professionals who know the student well and are familiar with his typical performance and behaviors.

As formal testing is often not possible, informal observations during functional tasks and interviews with those familiar with the individual may be the only means of securing information about fine motor and self-help abilities. Explore the underlying issues and barriers to successful task completion. Assessing the quality of motor skills, movement, motor planning, organization of actions, and interaction with materials in the individual's environment is critical.

When assessing a person through clinical observation, continue to be aware of normal developmental levels. For example, a child does not develop a clear hand-preference for tasks requiring precision until he is three or four. Therefore, it is not inappropriate for a two-year-old child to switch hands during tasks.

Environment

The circumstances, objects, and conditions by which one is surrounded constitute the environment. The environment is any and all settings in which an individual finds himself. Individuals with sensory integration difficulties frequently exhibit atypical reactions to the environment. These reactions can be clues as to the nature of the sensory issues.

Assessing the individual's various environments provides critical information regarding strengths and needs. Furthermore, this assessment provides an enormous amount of data regarding what environmental factors support or obstruct function. Gathering this information facilitates one of the first and perhaps the most important step that impacts interventions for an individual with sensory integration difficulties. See the Guide to Assessment of Environment on page 157.

Summary

Comprehensive evaluations include birth, medical, and developmental history, as well as clinical observations and appropriate evaluation instruments. An effective intervention program requires ongoing assessment to determine the appropriate established objectives and to revise and change them as the child grows and develops.

There are a variety of useful assessment tools that may help as part of a comprehensive evaluation. Some of them are listed in the reference section of this book.

Chapter Six

The Environment

Individuals with autism and other sensory integration disorders need strategies and tools that will enhance their ability to regulate their world and enable them to learn and participate in everyday life. Include functional and practical sensory strategies within the environment to insure availability throughout the day.

The role of therapists is to consult with teachers, staff, parents, caregivers, and, when possible, the individuals themselves. The objective is to provide interventions that will facilitate coping strategies that decrease individuals' atypical sensitivities. The development and use of appropriate environmental strategies require adequate knowledge regarding the process of sensory integration by all interventionists. There must be close collaboration with those extensively trained in sensory integration, such as occupational therapists. The level of supervision should vary according to the interventions being implemented and the level of expertise of all parties.

Environmental Effects on Level of Arousal

Dr. Temple Grandin describes some sensory input as painful and recommends that individuals with autism be protected from uncomfortable sensory input. If the environment is made as predictable and as comfortable as possible, the individual is better able to focus, learn, and interact. As the individual's skills and understanding improve, we hope that she can more readily deal with environmental stressors.

Be aware that people affect each other in the environment. How we move, how we speak, what we wear, and how we touch others impact everyone's level of arousal.

Triplets   *Jacob, Reanna, and Tyler are 5-year-old triplets. Although they were born at the same time, Tyler is not like his sister and brother. Tyler has autism and many sensory integration problems. Tyler's siblings do not understand what dysfunction in sensory integration is, but they live and experience Tyler's unusual behaviors on a daily basis. These behaviors can be funny, confusing, and sometimes scary.*

Tyler tends to put things in his mouth, so he is given special tubes to chew on at home. Jacob and Reanna never ask questions about the tubes, but they think it's fun to chew on Tyler's tube once in a while also. Sometimes, Tyler grabs one of his sibling's toys to chew on. This makes them angry. Jacob and Reanna are constantly reminded to put their little toys away.

Tyler has not learned how to talk yet, but he makes lots of noises. He sometimes sounds like a baby beginning to speak. He makes very loud noises that bother his brother and sister. The noise is most bothersome for them when in the car because it interferes with the music on the radio. Interestingly, noise bothers Tyler's ears, too. He walks around with his hands over his ears most of the time.

A note regarding Jacob, Reanna, and Tyler: The relationship among the triplets is ever- changing and developing. Tyler tends to wander, and Jacob has taken on the role of big brother. He is always ready to take Tyler's hand when he is walking away. Reanna currently appears to be less involved with Tyler, possibly due to his unpredictable behavior and his resistance to interactive play.

Tyler is fortunate to be growing up with siblings of the same age. He has constant models to learn from, and his siblings will be there for him when he's ready to interact. Jacob and Reanna will have a positive learning experience from growing up with a brother who has challenges. Even now, they are already showing signs of compassion and understanding of one another. At times, Jacob and Reanna see other children who may have something different about them, and they will ask questions about them. When they hear "just like Tyler," Jacob and

Reanna understand and accept this. They are learning to not be afraid of people with differences.

When providing any new strategy, including environmental techniques, one should encourage, rather than force, an individual's participation. The individual often may require increasing exposure to the modification. Structure and predictability are critical; therefore, changes within a familiar environment should be gradual to allow the individual time to adjust.

The effects of the environment build. One may be able to tolerate some environmental stressors for short periods; however, as the frequency, intensity, or duration continues, the stress can cause a sharp increase in one's level of arousal. Fatigue or illness may also influence tolerance levels.

Environmental Strategies to Prepare for Learning

Modifying the environment is one of the simplest and easiest tasks that professionals have found to be extremely effective in treatment. The table on the following page lists some of the more common arousing and calming environmental factors that can increase or decrease an individual's level of arousal.

In most instances, a calm environment facilitates attention and learning. Individuals in this environment are better able to tolerate the demands of learning and functioning.

Use caution in regard to interpreting an individual's level of arousal. An individual who appears hyperactive, or in her own world, may actually be in shutdown and not in need of any further stimulation. Shutdown occurs when the sensory information is so overwhelming that the individual basically tunes out any further input.

Environmental Effects on Level of Arousal

Observation	Arousing	Calming
Auditory/Noise	Loud, sudden noises or voices, changes in volume	Soft voices, rhythmic music
Visual	Bright colors, excessive background stimuli	Muted colors, minimal background stimuli
Lighting	Bright or fluorescent lights	Soft, natural lighting
Room organization	Cluttered rooms	Orderly rooms with clearly-defined pathways between furniture
Vestibular/Movement	Unpredictable, fast movements with sudden changes of position	Slow movements, rhythmic rocking
Tactile/Proprioception	Light touch, tickling, and unexpected touch	Pressure touch, hugging, moving against resistance
Temperature	Sudden temperature changes, temperature extremes	Neutral warmth
Odors	Strong or noxious odors (perfume, paint)	Soft odors (banana, vanilla)

Reduce Sound Distractions

Lower voices and decrease the rate of speech. Loud voices may get attention, but it is hard to "hang in there," especially when typical speech is perceived as shouting. This is an easy first step to calm an individual.

> *A parent told us, "Yesterday, after attending day one of your workshops, I tried lowering my voice when my daughter was having a meltdown. It worked!"*

Reduce sources of background noise—close doors when there is activity in the halls. Turn off noise-producing items, such as fans, radios, television sets, and even air conditioning units (when possible). Decrease the volume on the phone ringer.

> *At the age of ten, Pamela required a hearing screening for her school evaluation. Her appointment was on a teacher administration day to ensure a quiet environment. The audiologist's office was small and air-conditioned, with no windows. Pamela found it difficult to maintain her attention on the task. Her mother noticed that she would drift every two minutes, just when the air conditioner would click on. The audiologist moved Pamela to an empty classroom. Pamela was then able to complete the screening and passed with flying colors.*

- Use carpeting and ceiling tiles to reduce sound reverberation.

- Place tennis balls at the end of each leg to decrease the unexpected sound of a scraping chair.

- Secure foam with duct tape over the speaker to muffle the classroom bell or intercom.

- Provide a portable radio with earphones in noisy areas, such as a group home dining room, school cafeteria, or shopping mall.

Large earphones provide proprioceptive input while tuning out external stimuli. If the individual is distracted by the music and resists earphones, explore using soft foam earplugs. Another option is "noice cancelling earphones," which use electronics to actively reduce ambient noise.

- Form a "lunch bunch," a group of peers meeting for lunch in a quiet area. This is an excellent way of providing a calm, quiet environment while encouraging socialization.

- To decrease arousal, provide soft music at mealtimes to allow for a relaxing "dining" experience. Music that is 60 beats per minute, classical, rhythmical, or that incorporates environmental sounds is calming.

- To increase arousal for the individual who is lethargic or presents a decreased activity level, use fast music with an irregular beat.

Billy　　*Billy, a youngster with a diagnosis of attention deficit disorder with hypoactivity, was unable to complete his meal within the allotted lunch period. Fast, rhythmic music increased his level of arousal and shortened the time needed for him to finish his lunch.*

Reduce Visual Distractions

- Cover bookshelves and toy shelves with curtains when the shelves are not in use.

- Place objects in opaque containers to decrease clutter while facilitating a need to communicate by asking for wanted items.

- Remove or turn over visuals (such as circle time posters) when not in use to decrease visual clutter.

- Provide a study carrel or poster exhibit boards as screens on a student's desk.

Chartwell *Necessity is the mother of invention. At the Chartwell Center, teachers and staff are continuously problem solving, modifying the environment to help the students' sensory needs. For example, a nine-year-old student was having difficulty sitting in his chair at circle time in close proximity to other students. Even though he was seated on the end of the semi-circle, he would periodically hit the student sitting next to him. After several verbal reminders to keep his hands on his lap, one very ingenious classroom assistant placed a dry erase board between this student and his neighbor and used it as partition.*

The student was still able to see his classmates over the partition, but as soon as the partition was in place, he was able to refrain from hitting and to engage productively in circle time. Frequently, the student would look over the partition and smile at this classmates. Over time, the partition will be faded and the student will learn to engage successfully in group activities sitting next to his peers.

- Avoid excessive wall decor and displays that hang from the ceiling and flutter. These are distracting and increase one's level of arousal. The same is true of the interventionists' clothing, jewelry, and hair. Bright or busy print clothing, hanging jewelry, and long hair can all be distractions.

  A parent told of her child's distraction with the university logo shirts her tutors wore. The parent provided long black shirts for the tutors, and this simple modification enabled the child to pay better attention.

- Keep classroom boards clean; display only what is immediately relevant to reduce visual clutter..

- Use consistent color without patterns on the walls and floors.

- Ease visual orientation by using contrasting colors, such as a dark mat on floors in front of a light shower or commode. Contrasting colors during academics, such as placing a dark-colored paper under a worksheet, can improve the child's focus.

Lighting

Bright lighting and fluorescent bulbs often increase arousal level. The interventionist should be aware of her own position in relation to the outside light. Sun glare may cause difficulty for someone who is light sensitive, hindering her ability to maintain focus and attention. An individual who is light sensitive may benefit from sunglasses both indoors and out.

- Turn off unnecessary lighting.

- Use soft, natural sunlight and lamps with low wattage bulbs.

- Cover fluorescent lights with swag sheeting.

Room Organization

- Keep rooms tidy and orderly.

- Use dividers to define work or play areas; when possible, use an area for only one purpose.

- Arrange furniture with clear pathways. Poor sensory integration frequently affects motor planning, and this arrangement improves the ability to navigate by reducing visual demands.

Manage Vestibular Input and Movement

- Be aware of your movements and slow down—fast motion is stimulating to others.

- Speak to individuals at their eye level rather than having them look up or down. This facilitates communication because the individual can see the speaker's facial expressions and gestures.

- Consider limiting the need for individuals with vestibular issues to travel up and down stairs. When climbing stairs is unavoidable, travel when other environmental stressors are less.

Wes   *Wes was a thirteen-year-old boy with developmental delays and significant sensory issues. He loved working on computers, so his teachers did not understand why he did not want to go to the computer lab. They soon discovered that the road to the lab was paved with steps. By allowing Wes to go and come from lab a few minutes before the other students changed classes, other stressors were decreased, and Wes could deal with the arduous task of going up and down the steps.*

- Secure any flowing curtains.

- Explore alternative seating (e.g., a rocking chair) to provide vestibular input.

Manage Tactile and Proprioceptive Input

- Avoid very light touch because it will increase arousal.

- Approach an individual from the front rather than from behind so that she can see the touch coming.

- Touch the individual firmly for brief periods of time. Never force touch.

- Be consistent with where an individual is touched; predictability may help tolerance.

- Provide space for the individual. The end of a line, eating at the end of a table, and carpet squares during circle time may all provide needed space.

- Make alternative seating available. This can provide calming proprioceptive pressure touch throughout the day. See page 63 for alternative seating ideas.

- Wash new clothing prior to an individual wearing it. The softer the clothes, the more comfortable they feel. Labels and seams may be irritating. Cut out labels and let individuals wear socks inside out when appropriate.

Clothes   *Temple Grandin reports, "It took several days for me to stop feeling a new type of clothing on my body, whereas a typical person adapts to the change from pants to a dress in five minutes. New underwear causes great discomfort, and I have to wash it before I can wear it. Many people with autism prefer soft cotton against the skin. I also liked long pants, because I disliked the feeling of my legs touching each other."*

- Consider biker's shorts, tight sport shirts, or similar clothing to provide pressure touch to an individual who seeks this input.

- Install a hand-held showerhead at home to allow more control over the water.

Control Temperature and Odors

- Provide blankets for calming, neutral warmth.

- Provide neutral warmth in cooler climates by using flannel sheets.

- Avoid using plastic coverings on seating.

- Use sheepskin on chairs or mattresses as appropriate.

- Be aware of environmental odors and the individual's reaction to them. Adverse odors may come from food, cleaning products, classroom supplies, or toiletries. Use unscented products.

- Do not wear perfumes or colognes.

Perfumes *A young woman with autism was in an elevator filled with people going to a television taping. It was obvious that everyone had primped for the possibility of being on TV—even for a moment. However, the scents were noxious to this young woman, and she loudly remarked to her mother, "It stinks in here!"*

Additional Environmental Strategies

Provide a "Corner of the World"

Everyone needs an area to "get away from it all," particularly when wanting to relax from daily stress. This can be a special room in the house, a certain sofa, or a special chair. A "corner of the world," an area with minimal stimuli, provides a retreat for periodic breaks.

A quiet room, a classroom reading corner, an appliance box lined with carpet squares, a small tent, or a small child's swimming pool are a few examples. Incorporate various-sized pillows, beanbag chairs, gliders, or rocking chairs to provide calming proprioceptive and vestibular input. Eventually, the individuals may be better able to independently regulate their level of arousal by having an area to go to when needing to "chill out."

Alternative Seating

Various seating devices provide vestibular and proprioceptive input and, at times, boundaries.

- "Stuffed Pants" (See instructions on page 161.)

- Beanbag chairs

- Soft, stuffed chairs

- Commercial air cushions

- Commercial "swim noodles" cut to provide boundaries on chair sides and fastened with heavy-duty tape

- T-stools formed from two pieces of wood fastened in the shape of the letter "T" to create a one-legged stool (requires balancing skills and increases vestibular input)

- Therapy ball or large beach ball (stabilized in a shallow cardboard box to prevent rolling)

Seating   *Learning can often be enhanced by utilizing alternative seating such as a therapy ball. An article by Shilling (2003) published in* The American Journal of Occupational Therapy *described a small study of 24 fourth-grade students: 21 "typical" and three children with attention deficit hyperactivity disorder (ADHD). The children alternated sitting in regular chairs and on the therapy ball while participating in class work during language arts. Twenty-one of the 24 "typical" students and all of the students with ADHD stated that sitting on the therapy ball was more comfortable, improved their writing, and increased their ability to listen and complete their class work.*

- Inner tubes (To prevent injury, cover the valve stem with heavy-duty tape.)

- Rocking chair

- Hammock

- Glider

- Dycem® or nonskid material on a chair seat to provide additional proprioceptive feedback

- Thera-Band® tied between the bottoms of the front legs of a chair to provide additional proprioceptive input as a child moves her feet against the band

Kenny   *An OT and an SLP assessed four-year-old Kenny at home. His difficulties included a high level of arousal, frequent movement*

---

about the room, and a preoccupation with lining up objects rather than playing with and manipulating them. During the assessment, the therapists provided some quick environmental changes in an attempt to decrease Kenny's level of arousal and prepare him for task participation. This included lowering their voice volume, decreasing their speed of movement, and slowly swinging Kenny in a beach towel. A small booster chair provided boundaries.

When Kenny was ready, the therapists gave him a motivating puzzle task. The therapists held the pieces for play in order to facilitate communication and engagement. Within a short time, Kenny signed the word "more," a task he had only infrequently performed.

The therapists provided the parents with a home program, which included environmental modifications and sensory-based tasks. One such activity included play with and exploration of sponge alphabet letters during bath time. This activity incorporated a high-stress academic demand in a relaxing task. Subsequently, the family reported that Kenny had lined up his alphabet sponges. He had lined them up in the correct order, had been able to identify each letter, and had even self-corrected errors. Previously, Kenny's cognition was considered questionable, at best.

Obviously, it may not always be possible to place a child in a tub to work, but modifying a child's environment and embedding sensory-based tasks that meet his needs throughout the day can better prepare the child for learning.

When prepared, relaxed, and attending, the child is able to access his knowledge and can show us her true capabilities.

Positioning, Positioning, Positioning

When looking at the environment, think about positioning of materials. Individuals with sensory integration dysfunction tend to have low muscle tone with poor trunk extension. Positioning of materials in a vertical plane or upright position can help in many ways.

For the speech therapist, placing materials in a vertical plane (rather than flat on a table) and encouraging pointing or reaching can facilitate extension of the trunk. With improved posture, speech therapy benefits include increased voice volume, and improved breath control, endurance, and stamina.

From the occupational therapy perspective, not only is the postural control important, it also facilitates the development of the shoulder, arm, hand, and wrist that is needed for fine motor skills. In this position (extension), the wrist is correctly aligned to develop stability, and it supports the appropriate thumb position needed for developing dexterity. This in turn facilitates arching of the hand, which is needed for skillful manipulation of objects.

When working on the floor, encourage a variety of postures, including side sitting, prone on elbows, ring sitting, and side lying while propped on an elbow. Discourage "W" sitting.

Encourage working either in a sitting or standing position with arms and hands moving against gravity. Provide an easel, slant board, or book holder. Position materials to encourage slight reaching; this enhances the development of arm and shoulder muscles, trunk extension, and balance. Position objects on shelves, on the floor, or slightly out of reach.

Discourage "W" Sitting

Look at posture at desks and tables—elbows resting at about 90 degrees on the table, knees and hips at 90 degrees, and legs supported on the floor. When needed, phone books or stacked carpet squares can be used as foot supports.

Environmental Visual Supports

Many individuals with autism and sensory integration disorders are visual learners. Therefore, encourage the use of visual supports. Visual supports are concrete and static; they foster independence and responsibility, enhance self-esteem, and provide order, understanding, and organization to the individuals' often otherwise disorganized world.

Environmental visual supports include objects, pictures, symbols, and the written word. The selection of a visual support should be at the person's level of functioning and be as age-appropriate as possible. For example, a ten-year-old child functioning at a two-year-old level may do better when provided with a concrete object, such as a lunch box to indicate lunch, rather than a picture or the written word. However, be aware that when individuals are at an increased level of arousal, abilities frequently diminish and visual information may need to be at a lower developmental level.

When introducing a new visual tool, it may be necessary to demonstrate its use. This may initially increase the child's level of arousal. When the child is proficient, a visual organizer becomes a calming input in the environment.

Use visual supports across settings with all ages and developmental levels. Even though memory skills may appear excellent, stressors can tax functional memory, so cuing may be important. Effective visual supports decrease level of arousal, enhance ability to function, and minimize anxiety.

Supports   *At the age of ten, Pamela had to present a social studies project to her class. The presentation involved multiple tasks, which included public speaking and the use of props, both of which cause stress. Pamela successfully presented to her class by preparing a prerecorded speech. She was supported visually with a map that she pointed to as she played the tape.*

Well-positioned, clear visuals are essential. Avoid confusing and vague visual information. For example, visuals placed too high or out-of-range are difficult to use. Overly decorative lettering can distract from essential information.

The following are some of the visual supports that a person can successfully use in a variety of environments.

Personal Schedules/Calendars

Students should have daily, weekly, and monthly schedules. When appropriate, begin with simplified schedules and gradually increase complexity. Post the schedules on the wall, a desk, or have the students carry them.

Classroom and Home Schedules/Calendars

These give information about a day, week, month, or year. Be sure to sequence events within the calendar. Visually inform the students of changes in schedules (e.g., posting the word "surprise" can replace previously determined events). Using a photo can prepare the students for a visitor or scheduled events.

Visual Routines

Visual routines explain the sequence of an activity or task (e.g., washing hands, brushing teeth, dressing). For example, photos of clothing or sequentially numbered baskets with items of clothing in each can facilitate dressing. Expand this idea and use it with classroom activities (e.g., an art project). These children often learn to read by sight; labeling can facilitate reading skills and increase vocabulary.

Labels/Signs

Strategically placed labels/signs on objects facilitate understanding and the expression of needs. Here are two examples. During circle time, put a child's name or picture on a mat to identify which is hers. At home, put the child's photo on the bedroom door to identify her room.

Lists

Lists can be as varied as a shopping list, a list of class materials needed for the day, or a list of family members' and classmates' phone numbers. For beginning readers and visual learners, add a photo of each person on the phone list. Use dry erase boards or paper to easily compile written lists. Encourage the child to use a list to retrieve needed materials, call friends, etc., to facilitate independence.

Sensory "Cheat Sheet"

A sensory "cheat sheet" is a visual list of activities, categorized according to the provided sensory input. Post it as a quick, effective reference for both the individual and caregiver. Activities should be specific for the individual and easily embedded within a daily schedule. There is an example of a sensory "cheat sheet" on the following page.

Bulletin Boards

Bulletin boards incorporate finished products of activities that a child is going to participate in during school. For the older student or adult, bulletin boards announce current or upcoming events, community activities, and daily menus.

Color Coding

The use of colors can clarify and organize one's environment. Supplies needed for a specific class may be easier to access when they are all coded with the same color. For example, all of the supplies needed for art class might be coded blue.

A red stop sign on a doorway can often be enough of a visual prompt to stop a student who tends to wander. This, however, needs to be used in conjunction with a green "go" sign to indicate when the door should be opened to exit.

Joe   *Joe, a young man in his twenties, found it hard to verbally express his emotions. He devised a color-coded system to communicate to his mother how he was feeling. Joe wrote in red when angry, blue when sad, and yellow when happy. When his mother responded, she would use the same system.*

Sensory "Cheat Sheet"

Tactile	Proprioceptive	Vestibular
Dry beans, rice, or sand	Play the Hot Dog Game	Sit in a rocking chair
Work with Playdough	Pull a heavy wagon	Run races around the room
Draw with shaving cream	Push chairs under table	Play parachute games
Massage with lotion	Wear a weighted backpack	Jump on a trampoline

Visual Rules

Visual rules assist the individual by allowing her to review rules of appropriate behavior as needed. Pictorial rules (e.g., "Quiet Voices, Quiet Feet, Quiet Hands") strategically placed around a classroom are an effective way to self-monitor one's behavior. Personal rules (e.g., lunchroom and playground behavior) can be easily seen when laminated onto index cards and secured by a ring or in photos taped to a desk.

Visual Markers

These markers provide information about one's own space, activity areas, and boundaries. For example, use masking tape on a large table or an easel to delineate individual space yet facilitate working alongside peers. Strategically place furniture around the room to create boundaries of activity areas, using gates as appropriate.

Case Studies

One cannot underestimate the effects of the environment and the changes that can be made to help enhance students' participation and learning. The following case studies illustrate some modifications made to the sensory environments in these schools.

ACCEL   *ACCEL (Arizona Centers for Comprehensive Education and Life Skills) is the largest private special education program in Arizona. Formerly known as LATCH School, ACCEL works with over*

30 school districts and serves more than two hundred and fifty students with disabilities, ranging in age from three to 22 years. In January of 2004, ACCEL moved to a new campus which was renovated to be environmentally sensitive to the sensory needs of students with autism and other related developmental disabilities. The renovation project was conducted by Cook Associates Architects in Phoenix, Arizona.

The modifications that were made included the following:

- *Selecting nonprimary colors including sand tones and a muted green*

- *Choosing contrasting colors to provide visual definition at entryways to classrooms*

- *Painting stairways brick red instead of bright yellow to comply with ADA requirments without contributing to visual overload*

- *Using quiet, neutral-colored lighting. With the assistance of Cook Associates and the electrical engineering firm Diversified Metro Design Group (DMDG) of Phoenix, ACCEL selected a fluorescent light fixture manufactured by Lightolier. The fluorescent bulbs are rated 3500 Kelvin, representing the middle of the light spectrum between cool and warm. This light gives the most neutral outcome, reducing glare and reflecting colors as they are. Electronic (instead of magnetic) ballasts were used to eliminate flickering and reduce hum instead of electromagnetic ones. Using two switches permits adjustment of light levels.*

- *Equipping the fire alarm system with a chime adjusted to the minimum required volume*

- *Using of melodies instead of code calls or alarms for non-fire-drill emergencies: For example, playing "Raindrops Keep Falling on My Head" over the intercom alerts staff that all students and staff must come or remain indoors in the event of a lockdown.*

Informal observations to date appear to indicate that environmental modifications have positively impacted the behaviors of the students. ACCEL is now in the process of assessing the reduction in behavioral episodes and the variety of interventions that have contributed to this reduction, including a sensory-sensitive environment.

Chartwell *The Chartwell Center, a program for children with autism and related disorders, opened its doors in the fall of 1999 with the purpose of developing a school in accordance with nationally recommended practices and to serve as a resource and training center..*

The school is located in New Orleans on the campus of a regular education elementary school, and it operates a full-day school program with inclusion opportunities for children with various degrees of sensory and communication difficulty ranging in ages from three through twelve.

From its inception, this highly structured program addressed the need to provide a modified environment designed to decrease aversive sensory input and provide sensory supports to facilitate calmness, alertness, attention, and learning.

A Chartwell classroom is quieter than a typical classroom. The teachers and assistants speak softly; talking amongst the adults, at times, is limited; and music is played at a lower volume. The rooms are either fully carpeted or arranged with area rugs. The chairs have tennis balls on the ends of their legs so they don't make noise when moved. Visuals are kept to a minimum. There are no decorations or other visual materials that are not utilitarian. Rooms are maintained as neatly as possible.

Items are placed in containers, and computers are covered when not in use. The intercom is covered with foam and duct tape.

Rocking chairs, gliders, and chairs with arms and back supports are used to provide proprioceptive support, and trampolines and swings are accessible without affecting classroom routines. Students have access to a quiet area, and teachers are sensitive to environmental factors that may affect a student's behavior, such as odors and temperature.

Key elements of the Chartwell Center program include:

- *Making environmental modifications*

- *Applying child-specific sensory strategies*

- *Implementing a structured teaching approach*

- *Applying the principles of applied analysis*

- *Developing social-communication skills through interactive play and daily routines*

Chapter Seven

Intervention

Children learn through exploration and play. During the first year of life, infants begin with object exploration. A child achieves functional play when he appropriately manipulates objects. Symbolic play is achieved when a child is able to pretend that an object represents something else. Occupational therapists and speech-language pathologists should not overlook the importance of children learning how to manipulate, construct, and pretend, as these are the vehicles to learning communication and functional life skills.

Donna Williams, an author diagnosed with autism, said in her book, *Autism: An Inside Outside Approach,* that children with severe sensory processing difficulties often exhibit functional delays rather than cognitive delays. Functional delay refers to how an individual functions in life. It is about the capacity to act upon information in the context in which it happens. It is different from cognitive delay, which is the capacity to accumulate knowledge.

One can have an unimpaired capacity to accumulate knowledge (no cognitive delay) and still have a severe impairment in the ability to access and/or act upon that knowledge independently (functional delay). At times, we perceive the individual as having cognitive issues, when in reality the individual is functionally delayed.

Environmental modifications and sensory-based activities within the treatment cycle can help an individual maintain an optimal level of arousal and enhance the ability to regulate, organize, learn, and function. When individuals are ready for learning and skill participation, they often surprise us with their abilities. Expect more from individuals and do not underestimate them. Although not all-inclusive, the following strategies have worked well.

Treatment Strategy Guidelines
to Facilitate Learning and Communication

Use the following suggestions as a guide, along with the therapeutic approach and the treatment cycle, to provide a sound basis for intervention. As interventionists provide activities, they have to conduct ongoing assessments to determine the continued appropriateness of strategies and revise and change them as necessary for the individual's development and growth. Choose activities that are functional and appropriate for an individual's developmental level.

Be aware of the level of arousal and prepare for the internal and external environment through sensory integration techniques. Help the individual maintain the appropriate level of arousal by using yourself as a "tool." For example, when a child's level of arousal needs to be lowered, move slowly, talk softly, etc.

Motivation is critical. Gradually engage the individual by using tasks that are of interest to him in order to elicit participation and communication.

Self-stimulatory or repetitive behaviors can be the basis for the development of routines. Expand routines to increase engagement. With expansion of routines, try to increase function by replacing inappropriate behaviors with appropriate activities. For example, an interest in shredding paper may eventually lead to doing papier-mâché. The individual who is very interested in letters can develop motor skills by cutting, coloring, and writing letters. The one who has a high interest in lights may participate in flashlight play with others.

Initially reinforce communication attempts and then shape them over time. Acknowledge a sound with a wanted item.

Introduce new activities slowly. Observe the child's reactions for further intervention decisions. Do not force. Encourage activities according to tolerance level. Allow additional time to respond.

Embed easily understood communication into sensory activities. This can range from gestures, to one-word utterances, to complex speech. Providing information about what is occurring (or about to occur) helps the individual maintain alertness.

Pair sounds or words with motor actions to increase verbal output. For example, a child can be prompted to pair the word "jump" with the action while jumping.

Incorporate areas of need (such as academic and social skills) into motivating activities. For example, have the individual count blocks or read words that go with the task, etc.

"Sabotage," or the interruption of motivating activities, provides opportunities for communication. A motivating cooking task can be "sabotaged" by withholding an ingredient that requires a request. A child enjoying a puzzle needs to communicate if the interventionist holds the pieces.

Do not be afraid of "getting egg on your face." Be creative and explore new strategies. Failure provides vital information and ultimately assists creation of effective strategies.

Be cautious when providing prompts to facilitate task completion. Prompt dependency can easily develop. When modeling words, provide sufficient time for response attempts before remodeling. For partial and eventually full completion a of task, gradually decrease hand-over-hand assistance.

Vestibular Input Precautions

- Stop if the individual wants to stop.

- Stop if any one of the following occurs: sweating, color change in skin (flushing or blanching), dizziness, staring, change in breathing pattern, yawning, or nausea.

- Be careful with individuals who have a history of seizures.

- Never maintain a high rate of speed. Slow, steady movements are calming; fast, jerky movements are stimulating.

Sensory and Communication-Based Treatment Strategies for Children

When possible, these strategies are grouped according to their primary sensory input. The majority of items we describe are readily available or may be easily fabricated. Several activities require training and direct supervision.

Proprioceptive/Vestibular

Portable Ball Bag

- Place commercially purchased small, plastic balls inside a large mesh laundry bag (approximately 1/3 to 1/2 full). Have the child sit in the bag with the balls. Interactive play can include embedding language concepts such as in-and-out, color identification, counting, and social skills (exchanging various balls with peers).

- Have the individual reach over or up to retrieve or give a ball to a peer—this strengthens the upper body and develops trunk extension.

- Create a "washing machine" by gently shaking the balls while the child is sitting in them. This facilitates balance reactions and increases vestibular input.

- Hide various objects and have the child find and name the objects without looking. This is an excellent language activity, as well as a tactile discrimination task.

Contact Paper

Using contact paper with the sticky side up can provide a wide array of activities that are not only fun for many of the children but also provide increased proprioceptive input and momentary tactile input (for the defensive child).

Secure contact paper, sticky-side up, on the floor with wide duct tape. When the child walks on the contact paper, be sure to supervise him because his balance will be challenged. Activities on this paper include:

- Walking, with or without shoes

- Walking on tiptoes

- Walking backward, wheelbarrow walking, crawling, or "Follow the Leader" game

- Placing and removing objects and toys from paper

- Naming the objects retrieved

Art activities may include sticking feathers, crumbled papers, yarn, and other tactile materials on contact paper in order to make a collage that can be displayed after completion.

For the student who is physically challenged or just unable to manage glue, place a stencil cut from construction paper over contact paper. Encourage placement of a variety of materials to complete an art project. For example, cut an opening in the shape of a pumpkin from construction paper. Place this template over the contact paper, sticky side up, and encourage the child to place crumbled orange tissue in the cut out shape.

Take a nature walk and make a "bracelet" of sticky-side-out contact paper. Have the children find items such as leaves, flowers, etc. and place them on their wrists. Bending and reaching for materials encourage balance skills. Encourage directionality by indicating, for example, "There is a flower on your left side." Upon completion of the project, encourage discussion of items retrieved and the sensory components (e.g., the flower is soft and smells, the leaf is green, etc.)

Small pieces of contact paper can become a fidget to play with while increasing a student's awareness of his hands.

Towel Rocking/Pulling

Place the child on his back on a towel. Gently rock him side-to-side. Try pulling a child along the floor on his stomach or back. Singing during this activity can prepare the child for starting and stopping points and facilitates word completion. For example, "This is the way we take a ride, take a ride, take a ride..." As this is a very motivating activity, sabotaging by stopping periodically allows the child to request more. This is an excellent preparatory activity to gain attention (eye contact) and increase vocalizations.

Playground Equipment

Swings, slides, and climbing equipment on a playground offer unlimited opportunities for vestibular and proprioceptive input. Explore various positions on the equipment, such as sliding on the stomach, both forward and backward, and swinging on the stomach. When appropriate, consider indoor swings as well.

Racetrack Play

Create a track with tape on the floor. While the child is on all fours, have him "race" a toy car while staying on the track. This incorporates weight bearing (proprioception), movement (vestibular), and eye/hand coordination. This is an excellent opportunity to embed fun sounds, such as "roommm, roommm," "beep, beep," etc.

Creating a "track" in sand is an excellent prewriting task. Have the student move an item on a path from left to right (e.g., move toy farm animals along a path from the meadow to the barn).

Obstacle Course

Obstacle courses provide increased proprioceptive input and develop motor planning skills.

- Use home and classroom objects to create an obstacle course. Sofa cushions, tables, chairs, sticky contact paper, commercially available wedges, rolls, large blocks, mats, etc. are all useful. Have students create the course.

- Incorporate stories and language concepts. Include prepositions such as "over," "under," and "through" in the activity.

- Write concepts on cards and place them so that the child can see the word, hear the word, and perform the action.

- Encourage students to complete courses in a variety of positions such as walking and crawling.

Weighted Toys and Materials

Playing with materials that have weight stimulates proprioception. Stacking wooden blocks; organizing bookshelves; putting away groceries; and pulling, pushing, and carrying activities are examples of "weighted" activities.

- Add weight to materials such as cardboard blocks or empty food containers by using dried beans or rice in plastic bags. Be sure to seal the bags with tape.

- Reinforce classification skills by sorting a variety of foods. Have students sort the food containers into large brown grocery bags according to set criteria, such as freezer or refrigerator, fruit or vegetable, and healthy choice or junk food.

- Use a wagon or cart during block play and have the child deliver blocks and other slightly weighted toys to a building "site." Have the child load/unload and help build the house. Reinforce language concepts by pointing out changes that occur in the building (e.g., "The house is getting taller.") Following adult oral instructions enhances receptive language skills.

Fine Motor Tasks with Resistance

Hammer and peg sets, many types of pegboards (including those with lights), and puzzle pieces with Velcro® backing all offer resistance. Encourage social engagement by maintaining control of pieces rather than giving them all to the child. Hold pieces so the child has to reach across his body to facilitate gentle reaching, stretching, and midline crossing.

Thera-Band Activities

Purchase Thera-Band through an athletic supply store or a therapy catalog. Nylon stockings are a substitute, but they do not provide the resistance of Thera-Band.

- Encourage the child to hold both ends of the Thera-Band and stretch arms out to the sides—up and down.

- Place the band behind the child's back and have him pull to sides.

- Place the Thera-Band under the child's feet and have him pull up, etc.

- Encourage the child to hold one end of a Thera-Band and "squirrel" it into the palm to facilitate small muscle and hand-skill development.

This resistive activity facilitates overall large muscle strengthening. Naming body parts and position concepts enhances language skills, body awareness, and directionality.

Exercise/Group Sports

The following exercises incorporate heavy-work patterns and develop leisure skills. Vigorous exercise, twenty minutes or longer, three or four times a week, is calming. Mild exercise has no effect (Edelson, Stephen, n.d.)

- Walking

- Running

- Hiking

- Swimming

- Horseback riding

- Weight training

- Bowling

- Biking (stationary and mobile)

Horticulture Tasks

These horticulture tasks involve heavy work patterns that provide increased proprioceptive input, overall muscle development, and (frequently) enhanced self-esteem when an individual finishes a product.

- Gardening

- Planting vegetables

- Raking

- Digging

- Cutting grass

- Pushing compost barrels

Classroom/Home Chores

- Pushing chairs under desks

- Wiping the dry erase board

- Carrying books to the classroom

- Stacking and sorting library books

- Pulling a wagon of toys for outside play

- Putting away groceries

- Sweeping

- Vacuuming

- Setting or clearing the table

- Emptying trash

- Washing/drying clothes

- Sorting clothes of different textures

- Folding warm clothes

- Rearranging furniture

- Washing cars

- Cleaning wheelchairs

- Sharpening pencils

- Using hole punchers

- Stapling

Massage

We recommend training before providing this program.

Frequent professional massages, or massages provided by a parent/ caregiver who has been trained in infant massage, can be beneficial. The pressure touch of a massage stimulates proprioceptive receptors, which in turn, overrides a heightened tactile system and helps to modulate the vestibular system. Studies by T. Field (1997) found that children with autism benefited from massage therapy. The researchers concluded that massage therapy decreased touch sensitivity, distraction by sounds, and off-task classroom behavior.

Massage stimulates all the senses to help reinforce the learning process through the auditory (background music), olfactory (smell), and tactile (pressure touch provided by another) experiences. This helps make the individual feel safe and comfortable, facilitating the building of a relationship. It can initiate the process of developing effective communication. With appropriate preparation, professional massage can benefit the older child or adult.

Gentle pulling and compression of the arms or legs stimulates the proprioceptive receptors in the muscles and joints. The child who is seeking this input may offer his arms or legs to be gently pulled, pushed, or massaged.

Sock Massage

Placing a glove, puppet, or tennis sock over an interventionist's hand and then applying deep pressure strokes in a downward motion over the arms, legs, and back of the individual can provide proprioceptive input. Avoid friction and continuous motion over the same area. Do not force the touch—prepare the child in advance. At times, a child with tactile sensitivities will tolerate a sock massage rather than the direct physical contact of one's hand needed to implement a massage.

Mummy Game

This activity should only be implemented under the supervision of a trained therapist.

Wrap an Ace® bandage on a child's arms and legs from distal (wrist or ankle) to proximal (armpit or thigh). Apply pressure without constriction. Have the child wear it for approximately 20-30 minutes, generally 1-2 times daily. This provides increased proprioception and body awareness.

Pressure Brushing/Wilbarger Protocol

Implementing this program requires specialized training.

This technique, often used for sensory defensiveness, was developed by occupational therapists Pat and Julie Wilbarger. It is an intensive approach. Although often called a brushing program, it involves pressure touch, which stimulates deep touch receptors, and joint compression that stimulate the proprioceptive receptors.

Home Activities

Bath Time

Washing can help organization. With soap on a cloth, provide a few moments of deep massage. Incorporate language and body awareness by naming parts as you wash.

- Use deep massage on the child's head prior to, and during, washing his hair.

- Wrap the child in a large towel after the bath and provide deep pressure massage while drying. Follow with long body hugs.

- Apply deep pressure massage prior to hair brushing because this may help the child who finds hair brushing aversive.

Hygiene/Grooming

- Incorporate tactile input by using lotions or talc and by hair or teeth brushing.

- Massage hands and feet with a lotion.

- When using lotion, put a small amount in a person's hand and have him rub lotion into his elbow, wrist, fingers, toes, etc.

- Incorporate language by identifying body parts.

Bedtime

Tucking a child in bed, or placing pillows tucked around the top of the child's head, shoulders, back, and hips, can provide pressure touch and boundaries. Sleeping bags or heavy quilts can promote calm, restful sleep. Develop a bedtime routine and eliminate rough play (tickling, wrestling, etc.) before bedtime.

Tactile

"Stuffed Sweatshirt"

Tactile exploration is a critical part of normal development. Most preschool and kindergarten classes have "tables" filled with water, sand, dried beans, and rice. Some students are unable to participate in this type of play due to mouthing. Using "stuffed sweatshirts" (see instructions on page 163) prevents students from mouthing while they manipulate small objects. It encourages tactile exploration and the development of discrimination skills.

Additionally, placed on one's lap, this tool provides proprioceptive input. Encourage exploration and hide small objects to increase interest and develop language. Incorporate vocabulary and labeling of objects.

Activities in Tactile Substances

Use water, sand, rice, dried beans, shredded paper, Easter grass, packing material, and popped/unpopped popcorn (supervise as appropriate).

- Place the substances in small containers for hand exploration and in large containers for whole body play.

- Use indoor/outdoor sandboxes, plastic swimming pools, etc. to contain different substances, such as dried pasta, dried beans, or balls. Hiding and finding objects in substances facilitates tactile discrimination skills.

- Encourage writing or tracing in moist sand or dirt to provide increased proprioceptive feedback.

- Hide letters and objects and encourage the individual to find the letter and then find an object that begins with that letter.

- Encourage play in substances with a strong scent such as freshly opened candy corn or popcorn to add olfactory input.

Pouring Activities

- Use large measuring cups to practice math concepts (this facilitates fine motor skills).

- Mark cups with a heavy dark line to enhance visual perception of the measurement lines.

- Practice functional precision tasks such as pouring and measuring dried beans.

Exercise Putty and Play-Doh®

- Encourage molding and rolling putty or dough.

- Roll dough or putty into tiny balls by using only the tips of the thumb, index finger, and middle finger; roll or flatten on a table or vertical surface.

- Use small pegs or toothpicks to make a design or a plastic knife to cut dough.

- Increase interest by hiding small objects such as magnetic bingo chips in Play-Doh. This strengthens hands and fingers.

- Encourage vocabulary by putting objects "in" and pulling objects "out" of Play-Doh.

"Homemade Play Dough" in a Bag

This is a great activity for children who have tactile sensitivity. There are many recipes for homemade play dough. Each child can make play dough by placing the ingredients in a gallon-size Ziploc® bag and sealing it with wide tape. Encourage manipulation, squeezing, writing letters, etc.

Here is a recipe:

> 1 cup flour
> 1/3 cup salt
> 1 teaspoon oil
> 1/3 cup water with food coloring

Mix dry ingredients and add water and oil gradually. Add more water if too thick; add more flour if too sticky.

Water Activities

At a water work area or sink, provide large basters, plastic eyedroppers, sponges, etc. Have the child squeeze these tools to fill various containers. This facilitates the development of hand and finger strength as well as eye-hand coordination. Playing in water while using a variety of tools can encourage functional play.

Put Styrofoam® packing material into water and capture pieces by using hands, strainers, slotted spoons, or other tools. Facilitate sorting skills by cutting various shapes from the Styrofoam used in the water. Use sponge letters, numbers, and animal shapes, then have the child identify the letter, number, or animal captured.

Art and Finger Painting Activities

Have children finger-paint, using a variety of materials, such as paint, puddings, Cool Whip®, Funny Color Foam, or shaving cream. Add a drop of food color to shaving cream to add interest and encourage color identification.

• Secure a picture or drawing to a tabletop and cover with clear contact paper. Have the child "color" or cover the picture using finger-painting material. This can encourage the child's focus on the task.

• Practice handwriting by writing words in shaving cream.

• Teach letter sounds by placing a clear plastic board over pictures with the same starting letter. Cover with shaving cream and have the student write the letter while saying the sound. Push away the shaving cream to reveal pictures with that sound.

Sticker Play

As tolerated, place stickers on arms, hands, legs, feet, head, etc. as part of a game. This increases body awareness and identification. Placing stickers on and removing stickers from laminated paper or balloons provide opportunities for fine motor manipulation and eye/hand coordination.

Dress-Up Area

• Provide a box filled with hats, gloves, shoes, glasses, jackets, rings, bracelets, necklaces, and socks.

• Increase body awareness by using elastic bracelets and spandex tubes for arms or legs.

- Reinforce language concepts by asking the child which body part each garment goes on and what he wants to put on next—have him name the item and put it on.

- Read a story, play "dress-up," and "play act."

- Utilize an unbreakable mirror to enhance body awareness; mirrors can be positioned horizontally or vertically. Unbreakable mirrors are sold as camping equipment.

Ball Play

In play, children can roll, throw, bounce, catch, kick, or pass a ball. Using balls with a variety of weights, sizes, and tactile and visual components can facilitate coordination, motor planning, and tolerance of tactile surfaces. Two-sided sticky tape on a ball can facilitate holding and enhance tactile feedback. Reciprocal ball play is an excellent means of developing social skills.

Cooking

- Mix ingredients by hand, if possible.

- Use tools such as cookie cutters, sandwich spreaders, and rolling pins, all of which incorporate heavy-work patterns and fine motor manipulation.

- Make juice or lemonade and handle ice cubes.

- Follow recipes to incorporate math, reading, motor coordination skills, social skills, etc.

- Make cookie faces using icing, raisins, licorice, etc.

- For the individual who lacks motor skills, adapt electrical appliances with a Power Link® remote switching device.

Visual

Flashlight Games

Encourage the child to chase a flashlight beam or to follow it with his eyes. Ask the child to catch or step on the light. Take turns moving the light. To encourage language, ask the child to tell you where the light is by using such phrases as "under the table."

Shining a flashlight on a picture on a page or a specific toy can facilitate an individual's focus. Try using a flashlight with an adjustable beam (e.g., Maglite®).

Mirror Play

Practice songs with arm movements in front of a mirror. This may help some children see how their bodies move, where they are, and how their bodies are connected.

Motivational Toys

There are many commercially available toys that are motivating and provide auditory, visual, and tactile input. These toys also provide opportunities for learning and communication.

Handwriting

Handwriting skills develop sequentially. Imitating what the teacher has written directly following a demonstration is the first step in writing. Copying skills then develop from near to far. Copying a letter or word on the same paper is easier than copying from a book, and copying from a book is easier than copying from a black- or whiteboard. Independent writing is the final skill.

For the adult, acquired handwriting skills can be functionally embedded throughout the day for continued learning through personal correspondence, shopping lists, "things to do" lists, etc.

Positioning is essential during writing tasks. As illustrated on page 68, bent elbows should rest comfortably on the writing surface at approximately 90 degrees, knees and hips should be flexed at approximately 90 degrees, and feet should rest flat on the floor.

Incorrect desk posture can compromise balance, limit arm movements, and hinder accurate handwriting. Stacked phone books, held together with duct tape and placed on nonskid material to prevent sliding, can elevate a child's dangling feet and eliminate the need for the child to wrap his legs around the bottom of the chair for stability.

Handwriting Adaptations and Suggestions

Providing movement activities prior to handwriting practice can increase awareness of hands and fingers. Use short teaching sessions (10-15 minutes) and five-minute practice sessions. Increase interest by having the student copy from his favorite book.

Encourage handwriting practice in the vertical plane. Working on a vertical surface enhances the development of appropriate hand and wrist positions for fine motor and handwriting skills, as well as the development of arm and shoulder muscles. Provide opportunities to work in sitting or standing positions with arms and hands moving against gravity either at the board, an easel, a slant board on a table, or other vertical surface.

When writing on a slick surface (e.g., slant board), place the paper on top of a manila folder or ink blotter to allow for increased pencil control. Fun positioning adaptations can include writing or coloring while lying on the stomach and propped on elbows. For a complete change, tape paper on the underside of a desk or table and have the child draw or write while lying on his back.

Observe the individual's writing grasp and encourage him to use the "holding hand" to stabilize the paper. When pencil grip is poor (thumb is wrapped around the pencil, for example), explore commercially available pencil grips. If the pencil is held too close to the point, wrapping a rubber band one inch above the point can provide a visual cue for finger placement.

Be aware that atypical pencil grips do not always affect one's writing legibility; rather, look at the components of writing such as using intrinsic muscles (small muscles in the hand), positioning the wrist properly, and maintaining distal control. Using crayons broken into "stubs" can facilitate appropriate pencil grip, as the small piece of crayon must be held between the fingers and thumb. Provide coloring books based on individual interests.

Writing on a slant board can compensate for vestibular difficulties. Use commercially available products or make one by using a four-inch binder. You can glue a "chip clip" to the top of the binder or spray the binder with a photo- mounting spray to secure the paper.

- A strip of masking tape placed on a desk can cue a child where to place paper.

- *Handwriting Without Tears*®, a program by Jan Olson, has been successful with many of our students.

Pamela   *Pamela recognized all her letters; however, due to initial tactile issues, she refused to hold a pencil. The wooden shapes from the* Handwriting Without Tears *program were used as an alternative, and she successfully learned how to form her capital letters without ever lifting a pencil. Eventually, Pamela began writing and continued to use this program with modifications such as increasing the distance between the lines.*

Explore using the following sensory-based strategies as appropriate:

- Provide visual cues for writing by color-coding each letter stroke for clarity (e.g., 1st stroke blue, 2nd stroke red, 3rd stroke green).

- Encourage exploring letters of various textures such as plastic, foam, and wood. This allows students to "feel" the letters.

- Have the child write in pudding, sand, or shaving cream to provide tactile input. At home, reduce clean-up by using Funny Color Foam for writing activities during bath time.

- Have the individual form, trace, or shape letters from clay, WikkiStix™, or cotton balls for tactile input.

- Let children trace letters or words with glue and sprinkle them with Kool-Aid®. This provides olfactory input.

- Increase proprioceptive feedback by using a vibrating, weighted, or felt-tipped pen.

- Provide paper with raised or colored glue lines to cue for line usage.

- Place fine sandpaper under the writing paper to increase proprioceptive input.

Additional Adaptations and Modifications

Spacing and Line Usage

*   Use a decorated tongue depressor, a pencil, or one's finger as a guide—or have the student make a dot between each word to assist with spacing.

*   Use graph paper to help with spacing of math problems. Turn lined paper sideways to help with letter and number spacing.

*   Highlight lines to provide increased visual cues for starting and stopping points on a paper.

Copying

*   Provide larger areas for writing when appropriate. Research indicates that individuals with autism tend to write larger than typical peers at the same level.

*   Place work to be copied next to the student on a slant board, which is easier to read from than a horizontal surface. This modification will help students who have trouble copying.

*   Use a marker (e.g., ruler, laminated colored paper strip, etc.) to keep place when copying from a book.

*   Activities such as tossing bean bags or balls at a target placed at approximately the same distance as the student is from the board can provide practice focusing and fixing eyes near and far.

Attention Suggestions

*   Limit environmental distractions.

*   Limit visual distractions—use a study carrel when appropriate.

- Use a black mat that is larger than a worksheet to assist in visual attention to the worksheet.

- Attaching a surgical brush to the underside of a student's desk with heavy-duty tape provides a convenient hand "fidget."

Computer Adaptations

When appropriate, computers offer an excellent alternative to handwriting as well as an adjunct to it. Computer technology changes rapidly. "Closing the Gap" (see Resources) is a resource that produces a quarterly periodical and a yearly resource guide to current technology for individuals with challenges. This is an excellent way to keep current on what is new in software and hardware.

Weighted and Pressure Touch Equipment

Weighted items are garments and other weighted objects that are worn by a child or adult to provide proprioceptive input. This often reduces an individual's level of arousal during such demanding times as transitions and deskwork. See Resources for suppliers of weighted equipment.

Consultation with a trained therapist and proper adult supervision are essential when using weighted items on an individual.

Weighted Vests

Weighted vests (see instructions on page 165) should not be used by individuals who are pregnant or who have respiratory difficulties, asthma, or upper respiratory infections. We recommend that individuals wear the vests for 20 to 30 minutes and then leave them off for at least 30 to 60 minutes. One can purchase the vests premade or make them from hunting, fishing, or jean vests. Watch for possible difficulties caused by excessive weight, including drooping shoulders, difficulty in moving, mellowness, or lethargy.

Individualize the weight to each child or adult. Start with small amounts of evenly distributed weight and add or reduce weight as appropriate.

A person's size is not always an indication of needed weight. Vest manufacturers appear to recommend up to approximately 5% of a person's weight. Studies show that one should not apply more that 10% of a person's weight due to orthopedic concerns.

Additional Weighted Items

Lap Pockets

This is a device made out of cloth that sits over an individual's lap and hangs several inches below the chair seat. Use Velcro to close pockets/ channels on both sides. Add weight by filling the pockets/channels with dried beans or rice. Use lap pockets during sitting tasks.

Blankets

During nap time, use beanbag chairs as "blankets." For an older child or an adult, an X-ray vest can serve as a blanket. Keep in mind the precautions regarding weight (20 to 30 minutes on and at least 30 to 60 minutes off). When visiting a dentist, try allowing individuals to wear an X-ray apron for the entire duration of the visit rather than only during X-rays.

Weighted Sock

This is a long tube sock filled with dried beans that is securely sealed either by sewing or with a rubber band. Use as a "sitting pal" during tabletop tasks.

Weighted Backpack

A backpack weighted with books may help a student during transitions from class to class. Be careful to avoid excessive weight or having the student wear the backpack for more than 20 to 30 minutes.

Commercially Available Weighted/Pressure Items

Body Sock

The body sock is made from stretchable material. The individual can "get into" this sock and be enclosed from head to toe, providing pressure touch throughout. He can see through it and move somewhat while in it. The body sock can also be worn to the shoulder so that the head and face are free from cover.

Huggy Vest

This is a vest that provides pressure in the upper trunk and shoulders. A weighted huggy vest is one that combines pressure and weight.

Weighted Hand Patch

The individual wears the patch on his hand, particularly during writing tasks or fine motor activities, to increase awareness.

Weighted Foot Patch

The individual wears the weighted patch on his shoe to increase lower extremity awareness.

Weighted Collar

This collar, with channeled, weighted inserts, provides increased pressure to the shoulders.

Chapter Eight

Strategies for the Adult & Older Child

Although many of the activities in the previous chapter can be modified for the adult and older child, the following tasks are specifically geared for this population.

Proprioceptive/Vestibular

Can Crushing

To install a can crusher, mount it on a wooden board and attach it to a table with a "C" clamp. This allows the individual to sit while working. Can crushing encourages a variety of prevocational and vocational skills such as math, social, and money management skills (e.g., count the cans placed into bags, take the cans to a recycling center to be reimbursed, and pick up cans at various sites, etc.). This is an excellent heavy work task that provides proprioceptive input, as well as a repetitive "calming" action to complete the activity.

Ellison® LetterMachine™ Tasks

The Ellison LetterMachine (often called the "Ellison Press," see Resources) creates templates. These templates range from simple letters and forms to more extensive patterns that can be used to make pads, note cards, or boxes. The cutting of these patterns is repetitious and stimulates proprioception.

Woodworking Activities

Cutting and shaping wood, sanding, hammering, and drilling are some of the components of woodworking. Skills developed include organization, language, eye/hand coordination, and safety. This activity also stimulates proprioception through the heavy work patterns. Supervision is recommended as appropriate.

Exercise and Group Sports

Walking, running, hiking, swimming, horseback riding, weight training, and bowling incorporate heavy work patterns and develop leisure skills. Consider placing equipment such as a stationary bike or a treadmill at home and in school. Supervision is recommended as appropriate. Vigorous exercise 20 minutes or longer 3 to 4 times weekly is calming. (Edelson, Stephen, n.d.)

Household and Office Chores

There are many functional home, school, and office tasks that provide proprioceptive and vestibular input. Additionally, using these tasks throughout the week can enhance self-help skills, fine-motor skills, and attention to task. Mastery of these skills is also a great self-esteem builder!

When appropriate, provide such positive reinforcements as verbal praise, music, videos, etc. Options for implementation can include having an individual choose one task from two daily or posting a calendar with daily activities. Encourage discussion regarding activities for that day.

- When buying groceries, have the individuals follow a written or pictorial list, locate items in the store, and put away groceries at home. When putting away groceries, grade item weight, size, and placement on shelves at different levels to promote upper extremity strength and balance.

- Use cooking activities to develop upper extremity strength and dexterity, bilateral skills, and attention to task. Incorporate simple meal planning and listing items needed to prepare a recipe. Making the same item several times can help develop memory skills (i.e., what items are needed, what the sequence is, etc.). Begin with simple recipes such as mixing pudding, Jell-O®, prepared hot or cold cereals, etc.

- Cooking activities can incorporate mixing by hand, rolling, pinching dough for cookies, and cutting fruits or vegetables with careful supervision, which provides heavy work patterns as well as tactile input. Serve the "creations" to self or family.

- Load and unload the dishwasher, sort silverware and plates, etc. to develop attention to task and bilateral hand skills.

- Laundry tasks include carrying laundry to the washing machine, sorting, and loading into the washer or the dryer. Encourage using hand-over-hand motion to remove large items from washer or dryer. Sort (e.g., towels, colors and whites, matching socks, etc.) and put away clothes. Fold clothes, grading difficulty from simple washcloths and towels to rolling socks, etc. Hang clothes on hangers to promote upper extremity strength, motor planning, and attention to task.

- Develop upper extremity strength by sweeping and vacuuming the floors and emptying trash.

- Set and clear the dining table to enhance attention to task and bilateral skills.

- Increase motor planning and upper extremity strength by making beds, removing linens, and stuffing pillows in cases.

- Rearrange, stack, or move furniture.

- Sort and stack books and magazines.

- Encourage "tearing" old mail, crumbling in palm, and tossing into a wastebasket. Have the individual place stamps on outgoing letters and mail them. This develops hand strength and eye/hand coordination.

- Sharpen pencils, punch holes, or staple paper. Use manual, electric, or switch-adapted equipment.

- Wash cars, squeeze sponges, and wring out rags to promote balance and hand strength.

Tactile

Sorting and Categorizing

Sorting and categorizing incorporate academics, language, and life skills development. Sorting clothing for washing, folding, and putting away; organizing silverware in a drawer; placing dishes according to size in a dishwasher; sorting and rolling coins; and organizing food in a pantry are some examples of functional tasks that can provide numerous tactile experiences.

Art Activities

Ceramics and pottery incorporate hand-strengthening and proprioceptive input to hands and fingers, as well as develop self-esteem.

Paintings and drawings make wonderful note cards or holiday cards. Reduce a large-sized picture (black and white pictures work particularly well) to fit on the front one-quarter of a colored 8" by 10" sheet of paper. Fold to make into a card and add a matching envelope. Individuals can give cards as gifts or sell them. Great self-esteem builder!

Leisure Activities with Assorted Balls

Incorporate balls with a variety of weights and sizes, as well as tactile and visual components. Encourage activities such as bowling, catch, and basketball. Provide word lists, when appropriate, of the terminology used for these sports.

Water Activities

Swimming provides increased overall muscle strength, as well as an excellent leisure pastime. Washing dishes, hand-washing clothes, showering, maintaining a fish tank, and washing a car are all functional ways to encourage exploration of water activities.

Enterprise Activities

Several of the activities previously discussed allow individuals to experience "running a business." With adaptations and assistance, individuals can learn to run a successful retail business. Participation in "enterprise" activities varies, but it often includes the development of many of the following:

- Self-esteem

- Academics

- Social skills

- Communication

- Fine motor skills

- Job-related attitudes and skills

Some additional "enterprise" activity examples follow.

Dog Biscuit Enterprise

We recently became familiar with this activity through a teacher in Columbus, Ohio. She was kind enough to share her expertise in this "business." Here is her recipe for dog biscuits:

> 6 cups dry oats
> 2 cups flour
> 1 cup oil
> 2 cups powdered broth mixed with water (chicken or beef)

If the dough is sticky, add more flour. Roll the dough out a little thicker than a cookie. Cut into dog bone shapes with cookie cutters or roll dough into "doggie bagels."

Bake in 350 degree oven for 20-25 minutes. Turn biscuits over once during cooking.

Some suggestions for approaching this activity:

• Enlarge recipe and laminate for the student. Place the name of each item (e.g., flour) and the amount needed (e.g., two cups) on separate laminated index cards. Following the recipe, have the student match appropriate amounts to each item.

• Using the matched cards, set up stations for each ingredient so that the student can measure and pour the appropriate amount. The student then adds the measured ingredient into a main mixing bowl. Pouring and mixing ingredients together facilitates fine motor precision.

• Using a rolling pin, have the student roll out pieces of the dough. If the student is having difficulty keeping the dough centered under the rolling pin, provide a visual guideline by placing colored tape on each end of the rolling pin. Rolling the dough incorporates heavy work patterns and bilateral skills.

- When dough is rolled out to the proper thickness, have the student use dog biscuit cookie cutters or shape the dough into a "bagel." Have the student place finished biscuits on a cookie sheet.

- Bake the dog biscuits. Baking should be done by the instructor.

- When biscuits are cooled, label trays with numbers indicating the amount each package of biscuits will have (e.g., 6-8 in each bag). Have the student place one biscuit on each number. This will facilitate 1:1 concept. When each tray is complete, the student is ready to "package" the product.

- Have the student fill sandwich bags with the counted-out biscuits. If a student is unable to manipulate the bag and biscuits, support the plastic bag by using it to line a larger container before filling.

- Make "labels" by cutting out colored construction paper to fold in half on top of plastic bag. Labels can be commercially made and placed on construction paper. Place folded construction paper over the top of the plastic bag and staple shut.

You are now in "business." The biscuits can be sold or donated within the school for dog owners or to outside businesses. Some outside outlets include vet offices, pet stores, and small grocery stores.

Creative Cards Enterprise

Making greeting or note cards is a wonderful builder of self-esteem for students with or without sensory challenges.

This activity includes a variety of skills:

- Photocopying

- Cutting

- Folding cards

- Counting, sorting

- Tying/packing cards

- Selling/delivering cards

General Directions

- Encourage a variety of handmade drawings (black and white when possible) on 8 ½" by 11" paper. Drawings can be generic or holiday specific. See adaptations on page 114.

- Have the individual sign the drawing.

- Reduce drawing on a photocopy machine to fit on ¼ or ½ of a standard sheet of paper (8½" by 11"). This will allow for folding into a note card.

- Add any desired writing on the card. For example, recognize the work of the students by writing an explanation on the back: "This card was created by students from _____School. The students are are working toward their independence."

- Make copies on colored or white paper or on colored cardstock. Office supply stores stock a variety of ½ and ¼ fold card stocks with matching envelopes.

Holiday Greeting Card Template

Happy Holidays!

[Fold on this line first—drawing side out]

[Fold on this line second—drawing side out]

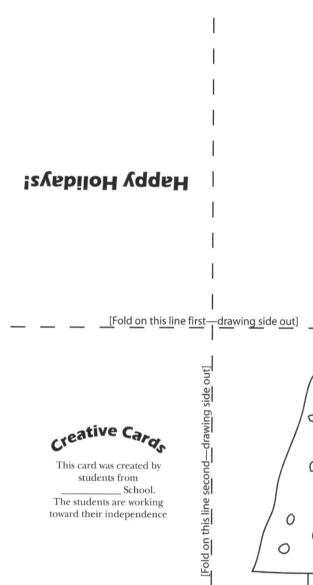

Creative Cards

This card was created by
students from
_____ School.
The students are working
toward their independence

- For cards that are ¼ paper size, place the reduced size picture on the corner of an 8½" by 11" sheet of white paper. See the template on page 113. For cards that are ½ paper size, placepicture on either the top or bottom half of an 8½" by 11" sheet of white paper. Adhere the picture to paper with rubber cement. This creates a template for the card.

- Fold into cards.

- Tie sets of four note cards and matching envelopes with ribbon.

Adaptations

Adaptations can be made for the student who is unable to draw pictures freehand. A student may be able to follow a simple picture if the task is broken down. For example, a holiday tree can be drawn by having a child copy a triangle, add some circles, and then a rectangle. The drawing template on this page can be adapted to other simple figures, such as a snowman. Other possibilities include tracing pictures or coloring in a pre-drawn picture.

If a child has limited physical mobility, sponge painting free hand or within a template can work well. A

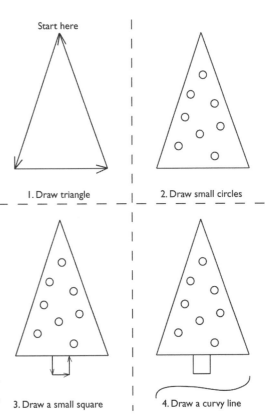

Sample Template for Drawing a Tree

magnetic template can be made on an Ellison press and put over paper on a cookie sheet. This helps hold it in place while the child paints. These paintings are "originals" and should be done directly on the paper that is used to create the note card.

The following letter is an example of one sent home to parents of students involved in this project. This is an excellent way to inform and include the family. This letter can be modified and utilized for any project, including the dog biscuit enterprise.

Creative Cards

Dear Parents:

With the holidays almost upon us, we have decided to create a greeting card "business." The students will make the cards. The entire class will participate and experience "running a business," from picking the company name, to making the cards, selling, marketing, and organizing the finances.

The benefits from participation in "enterprise" activities include the development of self-esteem, academics, social skills, communication, fine motor skills, job-related attitudes, and skills.

Watch for your "salesperson" soon!

Chapter Nine

Transitions & Informational Tools

Transitions

Transitions are the changes that occur regularly on a day-to-day basis such as going to bed every night, going to lunch during the school day, beginning a new endeavor or activity, having a new person in the day (e.g., a substitute teacher), or going to a new school.

Individuals with autism and a few other disorders are frequently preoccupied with sameness. Transitions and change can be difficult for some individuals with sensory integration dysfunction. Issues with shifting attention from one task to another, moving from one place to another, and waiting are continual problems. Providing clear communication, which results in understanding, combined with appropriate sensory input and activities, often eases transitions and waiting.

At times, transitions can be difficult even when the next event or situation is one that is liked and motivating. Establishing clear expectations and routines facilitates ongoing changes that occur naturally during the day at school or home.

Waiting is an activity that needs to be learned. Avoid waiting, especially when the child has not yet mastered this task without becoming stressed. For many children, free time is very difficult. At school, avoid down time by always being prepared with the next activity.

Teach a child to transition and wait by providing him with supports and rehearsing so that it becomes a learned skill that he can apply when needed. Difficulty with waiting and transitioning prevents some students from participating successfully in inclusive school settings.

One of the most successful and easiest strategies to facilitate transitioning is providing more time. A five- or two-minute warning or transition to the count of ten may be all that the individual needs.

Adjust the work to the time allotted for it, as some children become upset when they need to transition from unfinished work.

- Establish routines and use daily schedules in the form of checklists or picture guides for the individual to follow.

- Before unexpected changes occur, decide how changes will be shown on the schedule. For example, place the word "surprise" or "change" on the schedules and present these to the individual as soon as possible.

- Prepare an individual by telling or showing (visually) where he will be going and what he will be doing.

- Let the individual feel or hold objects from a schedule board (e.g., a spoon for lunch, a car for a trip, and a toy bus for leaving school). Provide visual icons such as photographs and words as appropriate. These are commercially available from Mayer-Johnson (e.g., Boardmaker®) and other companies.

- Use music and song to indicate transition; for example, singing "The Cleanup Song" can motivate a child to pick up toys to end an activity.

- Use a transitional photo book to prepare the child for a change or an activity that might be stressful, such as going to a new school or the dentist, by providing pictures of places and people, as well as activities that will occur in this novel event.

- Dim lights to aid in transitions by providing a change in the environment and a decrease in the level of arousal.

- Provide a slow loss in room lighting to aid bedtime transition with "glow in the dark" neon adhesives that gradually lose their glow.

- Make the individual an active participant in the transition; for example: "Let's take that book to my room."

- Use a weighted vest, pressure vest, or a weighted backpack to provide increased proprioceptive input as well as a visual cue to indicate transition, both of which are calming. (Please see directions and cautions for using weighted items.)

- A back pack that includes an assortment of favorite items such as toys, games, and edibles can help keep a child occupied while waiting.

- Encourage marching, hopping, or any type of little game during the move. This provides increased proprioceptive input.

- Provide steady, firm pressure on the top of a student's shoulder while walking alongside during transitions.

- Use timers to help an individual better understand waiting and to provide a tangible way to conceptualize time.

- Provide a carpet square to show the child where he needs to stand while waiting for his turn at the computer or engaging in an activity.

- Provide a "waiting object" for the individual such as a textured ring, key chain, a favorite book, a can of soda, or a calculator. A fanny pack filled with assorted items provides a "fidget" and can decrease anxiety during waiting periods. Also provide a "waiting card"—a laminated index card with a symbol or picture and the word "wait."

- Provide a "holding box" or special place to put things that they like to hold but which interfere with their participation in current activities. A "holding box" can help facilitate relinquishing of these items for periods of time.

- Strategically place a "Finished" box where the student can deposit work as it is completed. This helps facilitate transition to the next activity.

Informational Tools

Informational tools are pictorial or written assists that provide information for the caretaker or student to use. These tools facilitate consistency of care and integration of services in order to enhance the person's functioning.

Transitional Photo Book

As the individual transitions to a new class, school, residence, work, etc., a transition book provides a visual introduction. This tool informs teachers, caretakers, and supervisors about the individual's needs and strengths. It describes present levels of skills and lists favorite activities, likes, and dislikes.

The book provides a place to begin, helping to avoid errors and facilitating consistency of care from one setting to another. By providing information through pictures and descriptions, ideas and strategies that were successful or effective in the past do not go astray during the transition. In turn, potentially explosive situations or episodes of frustration for the individual and others decrease.

A transitional photo book provides the individual with an identity of his own by illustrating personality and daily routines. At times, the transitional photo book gives a voice to those who cannot speak for themselves and provides others information to talk with them about.

A transitional photo book can also be utilized by the student himself. When going to a new class or school, a child can review a book of photos to familiarize himself with the change.

A book with photo illustrations can teach a skill, enable the individual to review the skill, and help caretakers be more consistent with its implementation.

Fact Sheet

A fact sheet provides written information about diagnosis, specific strategies and adaptations, as well as general information about the individual. It enhances understanding and accurate interpretation of the person's behaviors and communication abilities. These informational tools are useful in the school setting, at home for relatives and sitters, and in the community at a work site. (See sample on page 169.)

Information Poster

Strategically placed posters, frequently including both photos and written instructions, provide important information regarding care and interventions for a specific individual. Posters let staff members (even unfamiliar ones) view specific strategies and adaptations. For example, the poster could show equipment needs, feeding information, and positioning strategies. A poster may display the sequence and steps of an activity that can be used not only by the caretaker, but also by the individual to aid in completion of a task.

Daily Communication Log

This is a notebook used for communication among teachers, therapists, and parents. A pre-formatted checklist may be ideal. It can be quickly completed to provide specific information about an individual. Pamela's Day (on the following page) is an example of a simple communications log.

Digital Photos

Digital photos convey information about an individual. They are excellent visual prompts to assist in communication among the individual, the parent or caregiver, and professionals.

Home/Classroom Handouts

Providing written material to reinforce classroom or therapeutic strategies clarifies information and can facilitate follow-through. An example of a handout that provides suggestions for both movement and sedentary sensory breaks can be found on page 173.

Weekly "Homework Calendar"

A posted written or pictorial calendar with a list of homework tasks reinforces and generalizes learned skills. Homework should be functional and fun. A functional activity at home can be to practice categorizing and sorting (e.g., putting away the silverware, matching socks, or sorting white and colored clothes for the laundry).

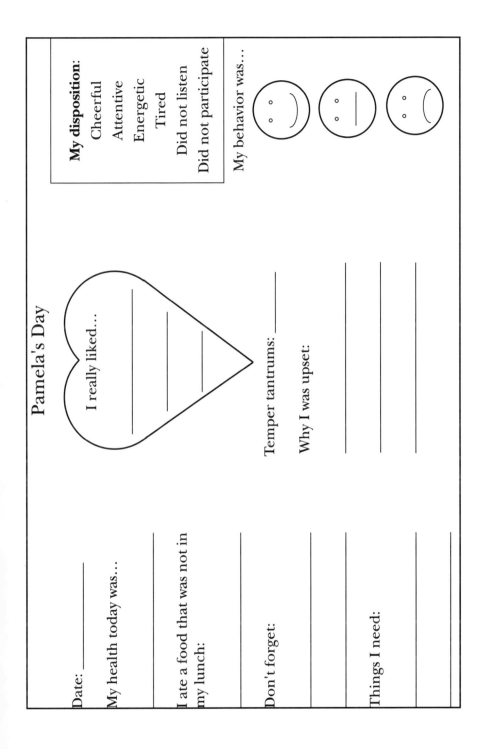

Pamela's Day

My disposition:
Cheerful
Attentive
Energetic
Tired
Did not listen
Did not participate

My behavior was…

I really liked…
_____
_____
_____

Date: _____

My health today was… _____

I ate a food that was not in my lunch: _____

Temper tantrums: _____

Why I was upset: _____
_____

Don't forget: _____
_____

Things I need: _____
_____

Chapter Ten

Oral & Feeding Interventions

The primary objective of oral and feeding intervention for children is to resolve or decrease sensory difficulties and to create necessary adaptations. For the older population, even though we now believe that changes over time can occur, a greater emphasis on adaptations is appropriate.

General Recommendations

Develop a relationship and trust prior to intervening. Consider the parents, teachers, and paraprofessionals as the main interventionists, supported by such specialists as speech and occupational therapists. In addition:

- Use transition strategies such as visuals and sensory calming activities to prepare for oral intervention or feeding.

- Introduce interventions slowly. Encourage, but do not force, participation in the activity.

- Use distractive games and interests (music or a favorite toy, for example) to facilitate intervention.

- Be consistent in treatment.

- Communicate frequently with other team members. This is essential.

- Revisit issues periodically with the same or altered strategies because improvements may be gradual and slow.

- Be aware of how the environment affects the individual's level of arousal and make adjustments as appropriate.

- Be aware of food or latex allergies.

- Incorporate modeling by a peer or caretaker.

Proprioceptive/Tactile

- Encourage the child to mouth toys when it is age-appropriate.

- Introduce a toothbrush as early as possible.

- Provide vibration by using an electric toothbrush, which can be less annoying to the orally defensive individual.

- Apply pressure to cheeks, lips, and tongue prior to and during feeding (i.e., young children may enjoy a modified game of "peek-a-boo," where pressure is applied to their cheeks and lips using a soft cloth).

- Wipe face regularly with a warm cloth if tolerated, using pressure rather than a light touch.

- Use the Nuk Massage Brush® during the day, prior to, and during, feeding. Place food on the Nuk, put it in the child's mouth, and roll it—applying pressure between the gums and cheek. Roll it side to side on the tongue. The child's tolerance determines length of activity, so do not force.

- Allow children to chew on functional, age-appropriate edibles and nonedibles to assist with oral-seeking behaviors (e.g., sports cup with a straw, "boat" key chain, gum, gummi bears, licorice, pretzels, etc.). Crunchy, chewy foods promote oral strength.

- Consider creating an "oral box" (see page 167) or fanny pack filled with appropriate "chewies." This can help address pica, which is an abnormal craving to chew nonedibles such as paint or dirt.

- Provide opportunities for blowing and sucking activities: blowing whistles or harmonicas, blowing bubbles, blowing colored liquid through clear straws, or drinking thick liquid through straws (applesauce, Jell-O, etc.).

- Set appropriate sitting posture at mealtime: head upright and on midline, chin slightly tucked, back straight, and feet supported. If needed, use boundaries in high chairs or other seats.

Taste Suggestions

- Introduce the most similar tastes first.

- Add new tastes in minute doses to familiar or preferred tastes and increase as the individual begins to tolerate the new taste.

- Place a new taste on lips—allow for exploration.

- Introduce a new taste with pressure (e.g., apply pressure to the tongue with a spoon).

- Give individuals control over the spoon, Nuk with food, etc. when appropriate.

- Provide well-seasoned and sweet-flavored foods.

Equipment

Consider using equipment to compensate for sensory difficulties:

Nosey cup—A cutout in the rim of this cup allows for drinking without having to tilt one's head back. This may help an individual who has vestibular issues.

Sports cup—The benefits of a sports cup include holding and squeezing it as a fidget and sucking through or chewing on the straw to provide calming input during stressful times.

Other equipment—Large grip utensils, weighted utensils, scoop plates, plate guards, and Dycem® or other nonskid material under plates are all adaptations that facilitate eating.

Food Suggestions for Children and Adults

Arousing	Calming
Crunchy	Chewy
dried cereal	raisins
apples, raw vegetables	bagels
crackers, pretzels	fruity chews
popcorn	licorice
granola bars	
Spicy foods	Sweet foods
Cold foods	Warm foods
drinks, ice chips,	hot chocolate drinks
Popsicles®	oatmeal

Chapter Eleven

Developing Communication Skills

The following provides specific suggestions to facilitate increased communication according to the ability level of the individual. Each section includes a brief description of the individuals for whom the interventions are designed.

Individuals with Severe Difficulties

Individuals with severe difficulties communicating tend to avoid interaction, are upset by the proximity of others, do not request their needs, and have little or no functional speech or vocalizations.

Suggested Interventions

- Gradually engage the child in a motivating activity.

- Develop routines from self-stimulatory or repetitive behaviors.

- Expand routines to increase the child's engagement; whenever possible, make it functional.

- Provide words to accompany actions and label objects, persons, and places as appropriate.

- Consider that rough-and-tumble play may facilitate engagement, especially with hard-to-engage children. However, this can be overwhelming for some. We do not recommend this strategy at bedtime.

- Interrupt or "sabotage" activity to reengage the child. This motivates the child to initiate communication.

- Teach basic action directives such as "Come here," Stop," and "Sit down." The child can be literally walked through these actions. Consistent compliance with basic directives opens the door for further learning across all settings.

- Teach communication by using basics signs such as "more."

- Use an exchange system such as the Picture Exchange Communication System© (PECS) or natural gestures (pointing or turning palm upward to request). Start with words that are the most motivating. See PECS on page 137.

- Reinforce communication attempts to encourage practice as the individual experiences success. For example, a vocalization that gets a child a wanted ball eventually may result in the child saying the "ball."

- Provide choices to encourage initiation. For example, a choice between a ball or a puzzle may encourage a child to make a selection by looking, gesturing, vocalizing, or saying the word.

- Pair a motor movement to a sound or word that is motivating to the child. (Say "Pop!" as a child is popping bubbles.)

- Encourage vocalizations through vestibular input and movement.

- Sing motivating familiar tunes and "sabotage" this activity by interrupting to encourage the child to sing along.

- Encourage imitative verbal behaviors during functional tasks that are motivating. For example, model the word "water" when the person wants a drink of water.

- Use "Motherese," an animated, intonation pattern frequently used to communicate with infants; it can be attention-getting when working with this population.

- Teach protesting behavior by presenting tolerable aversive situations for practice. A placemat with the word "No" may be touched to refuse a presented food.

Early on, consider pairing verbal speech with an assistive or alternative system. This will not prevent verbal speech, and it may decrease frustration and behavioral problems. In addition, this sort of system provides a functional communication system if the child remains nonverbal.

Individuals with Moderate Difficulties

Individuals with moderate difficulties in communication tolerate others if encouraged and supported. They display emerging communication and initiate mostly for basic needs and physical stimulation. They may have echolalic speech and have "out-of-the-ordinary" interest in symmetry and collecting.

Suggested Interventions

- Increase periods of engagement by using child-directed/ motivated activities that are adult-controlled. Controlling pieces or parts of toys (e.g., blocks or crayons) can be one way to prolong engagement. Use interest in symmetry and collecting to increase engagement. Slowly build tolerance for deviations in symmetry. Provide "sensory" breaks and discontinue the activity before an unworkable level of arousal is reached.

- Teach mechanisms to demonstrate protesting behavior. For example, teach the individual to use the word "Move" when the proximity of others is no longer tolerated.

- Encourage communication for purposes other than accessing needs, such as to share information (e.g., "Look") or to greet (e.g., "Hi").

- Set up motivating situations to encourage meaningful use of echolalic speech. For example, pair repetitive counting with a functional task such as tracking the number of times the child jumps on a trampoline.

- Use volume of speech to stimulate mitigated echolalia—the ability to extrapolate key words from a model. Model the desired speech by using and emphasizing, in a slightly louder volume, the key words the child should use.

- Continue to functionally practice labels (names of things) and action words as they occur throughout the day.

- Initially, teach phrase production of two words by keeping one word constant; for example, "Want cake" and "Want water." Conversely, others may learn by using completely different phrases, such as "Ride bike" and "Want cookie."

- Provide opportunities to physically experience concepts, such as near/far and front/back.

Individuals with Mild Difficulties

Individuals with mild difficulties in communication have sentence speech but have one-sided conversations, obsessions, and difficulties with social communication

Suggested Interventions

Social Stories

When describing a characteristic often seen in those with autism, Dr. Simon Baron-Cohen coined the phrase "mindblindness" to describe a person's inability to understand other people as having knowledge, feelings, intentions, and views of the world other than their own. He also pointed out that individuals with autism often have a high propensity for rule-based systems. Carol Gray developed the concept of social stories, which help to compensate for mindblindness through carefully crafted, rule-based explanations.

Social stories provide information regarding situations and appropriate behavior. They can address pragmatics and social behavior issues. Carol Gray has written a series of social story books with numerous prewritten stories that address a variety of subjects and situations. These stories may be used independently or as an outline to develop a narrative to fit a specific need.

Depending on one's comprehension, a social story may be presented through pictures, pictures with words, or words alone. Review new social stories with the individual and subsequently encourage reading the story more than once a day. Social stories provide opportunities for frequent review, thus enhancing one's skills.

The social world is very difficult for the individual with autism to comprehend. Social stories describe situations, experiences, concepts, and rules of social behavior in concrete terms, using a written or pictorial format, facilitating better understanding of the social rules and nuances that others learn naturally. Stories should be written at the child's developmental level. For example, if she is a beginning reader, use pictures and words. Simple wording with emphasis on positive behavior rather than on negative behavior is essential.

Barrier Game

Use visuals to aid comprehension and expression. The barrier game is an excellent example. Provide identical items to the individual and instructor, starting with two to four items, depending on the level of development. Set up a barrier, such as a manila folder, so that neither can see the other person's items.

Tell the individual what to do with her items (e.g., "Put the pencil into the cup."), while at the same time doing the task yourself. After the individual shows that she has completed the task, lift the barrier, producing a concrete visual of the correct answer.

Additional Interventions

• Teach ways to learn conversation turn-taking: when to start, when to stop, and how to switch topics. Use a prop, such as a ball, to provide a concrete visual for turn-taking.

• Make "figurine play scripts" with accompanied written activity.

• Use role-playing, which provides modeling, to increase social communication skills. Videos can also be used for this purpose.

Using Visuals to Communicate

Many people with autism and related conditions demonstrate visual strengths, especially when compared to auditory abilities. Various visual methods can increase communication skills. Use visuals to

• Enhance an individual's ability to learn to speak

• Help the individual to communicate using an assistive device

• Serve as an alternative system of communication

Visual information, in contrast to auditory information, is concrete and permanent. Once something is said, it is gone and cannot be retrieved unless someone repeats it. The permanency of a visual cue provides the opportunity for additional time to process information or have it available to revisit. An individual can use well-devised visuals to communicate with others. Over time, this can increase communication skills.

Visuals for communication can include objects, words, letters, or pictures. Objects may represent the object itself or a concept. For instance, a cup can represent a cup, or it can be a request for a drink. A toy cup can become the visual for the "real" cup. Pictures or words used in communication may include drawings, commercial icons, or photographs (digital cameras have made this medium very practical and easy to use).

Picture Exchange Communication System by Frost/Bondy (PECS)

This is a popular and easy-to-use visual assistance system to facilitate communication. PECS gives nonverbal individuals the first step in the process of learning how to communicate. At times, a nonverbal child may be unaware that she has the ability to communicate her wants and needs.

This program provides a step-by-step procedure and has a visual representation of what the child finds motivating. Once the child attempts to "go for" the motivating item, she receives the visual to offer in exchange for the item.

Initial physical prompting may be necessary. Decrease prompts as the child masters the skill and spontaneously requests an item or activity with the use of the visual. Introduce new visuals one at a time. Consistent use of this system helps master and maintain learned concepts.

As an aid to consistent use of PECS, attach pictures to a Velcro vest worn by the caretaker or put Velcro-backed pictures on strategically placed poster boards. For example, place pictures of food items in the kitchen.

If the child is interested in videos, strategically place pictures or the covers of favorite videos for her to use to request a specific video. Organize pictures by categories and place them in Ziploc bags or containers. Ultimately, the child progresses from using single words, to phrases, to sentences.

PECS Steps at a Glance

•   Determine what items are important for the individual, e.g., music, food, etc. Use pictures or line drawings.

•   Target one object. When the individual goes for the object, she receives the picture to offer in exchange for the object.

•   Gradually remove physical prompting as the individual masters the skill and spontaneously makes requests with the use of the pictures.

•   Introduce new pictures one at a time. Require the individual to maintain skills by using pictures consistently.

- Facilitate picture exchange by placing them on a Velcro vest or poster.

- Organize pictures by categories and place them in Ziploc bags, containers, etc.

Communication Boards

Communication boards, some of which provide voice output, provide low-tech to very sophisticated ways in which to encourage speech production or support an alternative means of communicating. Symbols on communication boards may vary and can include letters to spell words, basic words, pictures or photos, line drawings, or commercially available computer programs.

From time to time, parents and professionals have concerns regarding the use of augmentative or alternative systems to communicate. The concern is that a child may become dependent on the alternative system, stifling her potential for verbal communication. The literature has discarded this argument and, in fact, the opposite is the case. Visual systems increase a child's potential for speech production.

Visual or Photo Books

Visual or photo books are fabricated booklets designed to increase communication skills. These include pictures and names of items and are used to increase vocabulary through labeling. For example, a visual book might include a photograph or line drawing of a table with the word "table" adjacent to the picture.

Make photo books by filling several pages of a small photograph album with pictures that an individual can use to indicate needs and wants. Begin with one picture per page. As attention span and language improve, increase the number of pages and pictures per page. Have the individual turn pages to find certain pictures and name or point to them. This is a motivating way for children to work on expressive and receptive vocabulary.

Benefits:

• Labels and identifies items (e.g., favorite CDs or videos)

• Identifies family, peers, and friends

• Labels actions (e.g., run or jump)

• Facilitates responses to questions of "what, where, when, who, and how?"

• Increases verbal interaction

• Suggests conversation topics

• Provides a precursor to using an alternative system of communication (if needed)

Experiential or Communication Stories

These describe events through the use of pictures, photos, drawings, or words for the purpose of language development. Pairing language with an experience enhances understanding of the event or activity and provides more opportunities to practice language. For example, when asking a child "What did you do today?" try drawing pictures and providing words to describe the child eating, playing, etc. Using experiential and communication stories develops language skills— progressing from simple to complex development.

Chapter Twelve

Using Videos*

When working with the multifaceted difficulties that can affect individuals with autism and related sensory integration disorders, an intensive therapeutic team approach is the most effective. Parents are integral members of their child's treatment team. Their daily experiences result in some of the most innovative and beneficial techniques and strategies to facilitate learning. As professionals interact with parents, they learn new strategies that they can apply to situations with a variety of children. One powerful, parent-inspired technique is the use of videos.

David   *Tammy G. used a video for teaching her four-year-old daughter, Pamela, a child diagnosed with autism, because Pamela did not appear curious or interested in her newborn brother, David. In fact, she purposefully avoided contact with him. However, she was very interested in videos—especially those that included cartoon characters and music. For this reason, Tammy decided to "introduce" David to Pamela through this medium.*

The video was a brief segment showing David lying in his crib with Tammy narrating what David was doing. Pamela's favorite toy was attached to David's crib during the videotaping to further encourage her interest. Since Pamela enjoyed bath time, David was also videotaped in the tub. Shortly thereafter, Pamela developed an interest in her brother. This encouraged their relationship to develop.

The literature suggests that videos allow children with autism to learn in a medium that is more appropriate to their learning styles.

---

* Part of this chapter is reprinted with permission from the article: Kashman, Nancy, et. al., "Using Videotapes to Helping Children with Autism." OT Practice, July 3, 2000. ©American Occupational Therapy Association.

A significant number of them are visual learners (Grandin 1995). Frequently, children with autism have difficulties with eye contact and gaze, which are arousing. Using videos to teach a skill to children with autism can eliminate that added stress. Charlop and Milstein's study (1989) found that using videos was not only effective in increasing social communications skills in children with autism but also helped the children maintain and generalize the skills learned.

Videos are predictable, can be tailored to specific interests, and allow multiple viewings. Videos let children with autism work through some of their difficulties and phobias.

Luscre and Center's study (1996) used video training to reduce "dental phobia" in children with autism. They used three basic techniques: calming toys/activities throughout the exam, video viewing followed by practice of the procedure in a simulated setting, and the child's favorite reinforcers/rewards. Results were very favorable.

Children with autism exhibit "tunnel vision" (Lovaas, Schreibman, Koegel, and Rhem 1971), which is the ability to focus on one stimulus or part of a "whole." Set in an optimal environment, videos offer learning tailored to fit the individual's needs.

In our practice, we use videos for a variety of reasons, from assessment to intervention. Used as an adjunct to an evaluation, videotaping the child can offer the opportunity to more accurately assess a child's skill level by observing the child within his natural environment without the impact of the examiner. Assessed skills may include social, communication, motor, cognitive/academic, and self-help.

Children with autism exhibit sensory processing difficulties that are frequently challenging to assess in a clinical setting. During the natural course of a day, videos can provide insight into a child's ability to process sensory information. A child's reactions to the world around him, his level of arousal, and any avoiding or seeking behaviors may appear.

The team can assess his play skills, need for personal space, sociability, and response to touch.

Gross and fine motor skills (such as general posture, balance, fluidity of movement; manipulation; spatial perception; and motor planning skills) are seen as the individual navigates his environment. Additionally, videos provide an effective means of documenting progress over time. The observer can note the child's attention span and stamina by the length of time he remains on a task and his ability to transition and shift his attention. Videos often provide us with a view of the antecedents when self-injurious or stereotypic behaviors are issues.

Observation of the environment is necessary for future intervention. Modifying the environment is often the easiest and quickest way to facilitate change. As the effect of the environment builds over time, simple changes can help maintain a child's appropriate level of arousal needed for intervention.

Things to look at in the environment include the noise level and the child's reaction to it. Visual stimuli, which include wall decor and clutter, can easily be modified if the child appears to react to it. When looking at toys or equipment, note if there are special toys he seeks or avoids.

Viewing others in the child's environment, their interaction, and the child's response, provides information to the caretakers and allows for ongoing intervention. As interventionists, we can assess our own interactions and capture reactions and behaviors that we may miss when we are in the middle of a session.

Videos also facilitate the development of goals and objectives. Intervention videos can enhance individuals' abilities to learn about themselves and the world around them. Videos may be commercial videos or child-specific.

Homemade, child-specific intervention videos facilitate the development of a variety of skills, provide "drills" during extended school breaks to avoid regression of achieved skills, and prepare the child for transitions. The older individual may benefit from videos for prevocational or vocational training and social skills. See the following guidelines for suggestions on producing child-specific videos.

Guidelines for the Production of Intervention Videos

- Develop videos by a thorough analysis of an individual's needs and interests. A task analysis of the targeted skill is recommended.

- Prepare a script prior to taping. Carol Gray's social stories are helpful for preparing scripts.

- Imbed challenging activities into familiar and interesting tasks such as handwriting and bathing.

- Be aware of an individual's attention span. Try to expand the attention span by including "grabbers" such as music and movement.

- Speak clearly and eliminate nonessential speech. Allow time for responses between activities.

- Repeat activities more than once, if necessary.

- Simplify video scenes by filtering out extraneous objects, sounds, and movements that can clutter and confuse the individual.

- Isolate the skill to develop and provide prompts. Label objects, persons, and actions as appropriate.

- Provide a variety of examples to help the learner generalize the lesson.

- Keep manipulatives and objects used in the video handy, so that the individual can use them while watching the video.

- Increase learning through interaction or practice with an instructor or peer during, in between, or after the video.

- Reintroduce all forms of stimulation because some people are not interested in videos. The individual may develop an interest over time. Never force; just encourage.

- Introduce "real people" slowly—many children will initially only watch cartoon videos. Peers and familiar persons or objects can be especially interesting.

- Do not overuse the video to the point of boredom.

- Obtain prior consent of parent or caregiver to resolve confidentiality issues.

Chapter Thirteen

Teaming Case Studies

Taking an team approach to implementing sensory and communication strategies requires close coordination, mutual respect, and a willingness to improvise. The following case studies illustrate how the benefits of a team approach reinforce and enhance the knowledge, skills, and abilities of the team members, providing better and more effective treatment. The team's ability to improvise proved particularly important. Because of the location—El Salvador—the team did not have access to a wide range of therapy supplies and equipment.

Those involved had not worked together previously, and working effectively as members of a team requires training and practice. The first step was to orient the team members who would evaluate and treat affected children. An introductory seminar for approximately eighty therapists, teachers, parents, and administrators included an overview of sensory integration and communication difficulties, functional intervention, and teaming to provide a comprehensive intervention plan for the home and classroom.

Teaming, at first glance, may appear to be a simple concept and an easy skill to develop. The concept of teaming is not new, but it is often difficult to implement. Experience has demonstrated that effective teaming is an ongoing and always evolving process. When teaming, the development of new techniques and strategies is continuous as one learns from the child, the family, caretakers, and other interventionists. The result of working together is synergistic, as several "heads and hands together" often elicit more creative interventions.

Lack of teaming hinders communication and may result in treating a child segmentally rather than holistically. For example, a parent reported that several interventionists worked with her child but had never communicated with each other. As a result of the seminar in

El Salvador, everyone had a better understanding of how to work as members of a team. Subsequently, the group reformed into small teams for problem solving, strategizing, and treatment.

Christina   *The success of a team approach was evident when treating Christina, a three-year-old girl diagnosed with a rare genetic disorder called "trisomy eight." She was receiving physical therapy, and her mother wanted additional functional strategies to embed in Christina's day.*

A brief assessment included parental questioning and "play" with Christina by a team composed of a special education teacher, an OT, and an SLP. The child's mother, sister, and nanny also participated, providing observations of Christina's behavior since birth.

Christina, a charming and personable child, presented overall hypotonicity with decreased strength and endurance. These difficulties impacted her general posture, movements, and communication. Although Christina's speech articulation was clear, verbalizing was an effort. Her low volume and brief, infrequently produced phrases hindered her communication.

Christina's sitting balance was unstable. Her low tone caused her to "crash" into those supporting her. To provide support for sitting, the use of "stuffed pants" was considered to provide boundaries and postural support.

After an exchange of ideas and information, the team suggested:

- Using music to motivate Christina to increase vocalization, vocabulary, and participation in motor tasks

- Placing many of her toys on a vertical plane slightly at or above eye level to facilitate trunk extension, develop upper body strength, and increase voice volume

- Encouraging Christina to play with a variety of tactile substances, such as dry beans, rice, or sand, to provide hand-strengthening games and to give her an increased opportunity to investigate new textures

- Using alternative seating, such as "stuffed pants," to provide additional postural support

The Orphanage

The team visited an orphanage for children with special needs. The residents' ages ranged from birth to adult. The orphanage did not have any occupational or speech language therapists, but it did have physical therapists, who were quite adept at fabricating seating adaptations. They used readily available but low cost materials, such as Styrofoam® and cardboard boxes.

The visiting occupational therapist teamed with the physical therapists to develop appropriate strategies and identify needed interventions. Together, they developed functional requirements for a dynamic thumb abductor splint for one of the children. The speech therapist shared with the staff therapists simple but effective communication strategies, such as providing more time for a child with autism to respond.

Anna   *With her permission, the team made a video of Anna, a bright, articulate, thirty-eight-year-old woman who was severely affected by juvenile arthritis. Amazingly, although her fingers were severely contracted, Anna had sufficient grasp to create beautiful, woven, infant headbands. Due to her dependency in the area of self-help, the therapists requested exploring adaptations to facilitate independence in feeding. Making a video enabled the team members to consult with specialists who were not able to travel to the remote location. This enabled the team to provide Anna with adaptive equipment. She is now able to feed herself.*

Conclusions

Therapists are most effective when they work in teams, and teams are most effective when the members are creative, take risks, and learn from each other.

Appendicies

Sensory Integration Disorders

Dysfunction in sensory integration affects a wide variety of people, including a significant percentage of individuals who are also affected by other developmental conditions. Those other conditions sometimes exacerbate or mask sensory issues. Therapists should therefore be alert to the possibility of coexisting conditions when assessing and treating people with sensory dysfunctions. This appendix briefly describes a number of developmental conditions that may coexist with dysfunction in sensory integration.

The Autism Spectrum

Autism is one of several disorders that falls under the umbrella of pervasive developmental disorder (PDD). These are generally recognized as involving three impairments: language and communication, social interaction, and imaginative play—including restricted interests and activities.

While physicians look for these three hallmarks to diagnose autism, there are other symptoms that are common, but by no means universal: odd or repetitive behaviors, lack of eye contact, impaired gait and posture, sensory difficulties, and problems with attention/motivation. As our knowledge and understanding of individuals with autism has grown, we increasingly realize that many individuals go through life experiencing difficulties with sensory integration. In most cases, these sensory difficulties interfere with the person's ability to interact with (and make sense of) his world.

Autism is a lifelong disability that typically appears during the first three years of a child's life. We now call autism a spectrum disorder (ASD)—the symptoms and behaviors can present themselves in a wide variety of combinations, ranging from mild to severe. Severe behaviors can include self-injury. In addition to autism, many other diagnoses involve sensory integration difficulties.

Asperger's Syndrome

Individuals with Asperger's syndrome typically do not present with delays in language acquisition or cognitive development. However, they do exhibit difficulties with social behaviors and have tendencies toward obsessive interests.

Pervasive Developmental Disorder Not Otherwise Specified (PDD/NOS)

These individuals exhibit many of the symptoms of autism, but not all. The symptoms may be less severe than those of autism, but they do not meet the criteria for the diagnosis of other disorders, such as mental retardation or attention deficit hyperactivity disorder.

Childhood Disintegrative Disorder

This is a rare variation of PDD. A marked loss of communication, social, and self-help skills, and sometimes motor skills, follows a period of at least two years of normal development. This primarily affects boys.

Rett Syndrome

This syndrome is a movement disorder characterized by stereotypic hand wringing and mental retardation. It presents itself following a six-to-eighteen-month period of normal development. Associated deficits include loss of language and motor skills and self-injurious behavior. Rett syndrome generally occurs only in females. A regression in cognition and behavior, social and motor skills is noted throughout the lifetime of those affected.

Disorders with Autistic Features

Landau-Kleffner Syndrome

This syndrome causes a rapid loss of language between the ages of three and seven, with clinical seizures in up to eighty percent of cases. These seizures have a direct impact on language loss. The individuals first lose their ability to comprehend (i.e., receptive speech) and then their ability to speak (i.e., expressive speech), with changes occurring gradually or suddenly.

Characteristics include failure to respond to sounds, pain insensitivity, aggression, poor eye contact, insistence on sameness, and sleep problems. It is twice as common in males as in females.

Fragile X

Individuals with this disorder often present with repetitive motor behaviors, hypersensitivity to sound, hyposensitivity or hypersensitivity to oral or facial stimulation, and mild to severe cognitive delays.

Neurofibromatosis

This hereditary disorder involves the development of tumors of the peripheral nerves. Location of the tumors can affect neuromotor, sensory, and/or intellectual functioning.

Tuberous Sclerosis

This is a congenital disease characterized by tumors of the lateral ventricle and sclerotic patches on the brain. Progressive cognitive dysfunction and seizures occur.

Prader-Willi Syndrome

This syndrome is characterized by obsession with food and impulsive eating. Delays in language and motor development occur. Symptoms also include infant feeding problems, sleep disturbances, skin picking, temper tantrums, tactile hyposensitivity, and poor muscle tone. Most individuals with this syndrome have cognitive impairment.

Williams Syndrome

This is a genetic disorder characterized by mild mental retardation and unique, pixie-like facial features. Behaviors include developmental and language delays, difficulties with gross motor skills, hypersensitivity to sounds, picky eating, and perseveration. This population is very sociable.

Hyperlexia

This disorder includes an intense fascination with letters, numbers, patterns, and logos. The individuals have a self-taught precocious ability to read (not necessarily with comprehension), spell, write, or compute, usually before the age of five. The individuals have difficulty developing language and communication skills. They often exhibit unusual behaviors or interests. There is less effect on social interactions than experienced with autism.

Conditions With Sensory Integration Difficulties

The criteria for diagnosis of the following impairments do not necessarily include difficulties with sensory integration. However, neuromuscular limitations, developmental delays, or medical issues can cause either primary or secondary sensory integration impairments to occur.

Cerebral Palsy

Professionals often describe cerebral palsy as a sensory-motor disorder. Usually, most of the emphasis in treatment is directed toward the motor and movement difficulties. Frequently, individuals with cerebral palsy exhibit problems with sensory integration that are primary or secondary in nature. The primary deficits are those that occur concurrently with the movement disorder. Secondary deficits are those that are the result of the movement disorder.

Down Syndrome

This is the most common chromosomal abnormality. Most areas of development are affected to a lesser or greater degree, including cognition, motor skills, communication, and sensory skills.

Others

Prematurity, attention deficit disorders, behavior disorders, learning disabilities, Alzheimer's disease, chronic illness, fetal alcohol syndrome, and traumatic brain injury can cause difficulties in processing sensory information from the environment and one's body. This can cause difficulties in attention, behavior, learning, speech development, and movement patterns. At times, the symptoms seen in the individuals suffering from one of these disorders are due to sensory integration problems.

Guide to Assessment of Environment

The following is an informal guide developed to assess a classroom environment. This may be modified for use in home and work settings.

Name _____

Date_____

Area_____

Examiner_____

Directions: Investigate the various sensory experiences of your classroom. Observations should reflect naturally occurring events, including physical surroundings and other individuals in the situation. Environmental modifications should be reasonable and practical. Some examples are provided for clarity.

	Observation	Needs

I. Room Organization

    A. Overall safety of room

    B. Ease of movement around area

    C. Orderliness and efficiency of room

       (e.g., clutter, everything in its place)

    D. Existing modifications

    E. Individual reactions

II. Noise Level

A. Overall noise level

B. Unexpected noises

    1. Cause (e.g., phone, bell, etc.)

    2. Frequency

    3. Duration

    4. Intensity (how loud)

C. Existing modifications

D. Individual reaction

    1. Immediate

    2. Delayed (e.g., escalates)

    3. Degree (mild, moderate, or severe)

III. Visual Stimuli

A. Type of visual stimuli

    1. Static or moving

    2. Patterns or colors

B. Quantity of visual stimuli

C. Lighting (e.g., shadows, fluorescent, or natural)

D Existing modifications

E. Individual reaction

    1. Immediate

Observation	Needs

2. Delayed (e.g., escalates)

3. Degree (mild, moderate, or severe)

IV. Odors

   A. Noticeable odors
(e.g., from meals, cooking, art activities, etc.)

   B. Existing modifications

   C. Individual reaction

      1. Immediate or delayed (e.g., escalates)

      2. Degree (mild, moderate, or severe)

V. Temperature

   A. Temperature of area

   B. Changes in temperature

   C. Existing modifications

   D. Individual reaction

      1. Immediate

      2. Delayed (e.g., escalates)

      3. Degree (mild, moderate, or severe)

VI. Available Equipment (Tactile, Proprioceptive, and Vestibular)

   A. Gross motor (e.g., swings, exercise equipment)

   B. Seating (e.g., gliders, rocking chair, beanbag chair)

   C. Effective use of equipment

   D. Modifications implemented

   E. Individual reaction

VII. Environmental Visual Supports

   A. Current visual supports available

   B. Individual reactions

VIII.   Others in the environment (e.g., caretakers, parents, teachers, and peers)

   A. Current visual supports available

   B. Individual reactions

"Stuffed Pants"

It is often quite difficult to appropriately position the severely challenged individual. Although there are fine pieces of equipment available for purchase, they are often quite expensive and, at times, bulky and large. Using cushions or pillows can sometimes provide support.

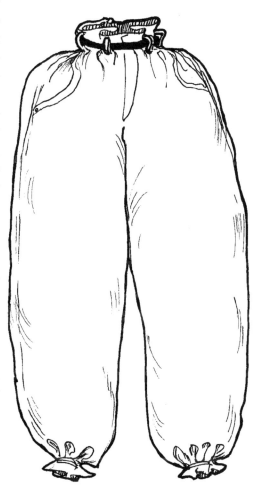

However, these frequently slip and often do not provide adequate support. Use "stuffed pants" for positioning a severely challenged individual in supine, side lying, prone, or unsupported sitting. Individuals with sensory processing difficulties often seek increased proprioceptive input. A beanbag chair or "stuffed pants" can provide this input.

"Stuffed pants" are easily made from sweatpants or other soft material and are stuffed with foam or other malleable material. Securely close the legs and waist of the pants with large rubber bands. Not closing them permanently allows for washing and appropriate sanitary care. Use caution when providing these pants to individuals who mouth objects.

"Stuffed Sweatshirt"

Tactile exploration is a critical part of normal development. Most preschool and kindergarten classes have "tables" filled with water, sand, dried beans, and rice. Some students are unable to participate in this type of play due to mouthing. Using "stuffed sweatshirts" prevents students from mouthing while they manipulate small objects. It encourages tactile exploration and the development of discrimination skills. Additionally, placed on one's lap, this tool provides proprioceptive input. Encourage exploration and hide small objects to increase interest and develop language. Incorporate vocabulary and labeling of objects.

The "stuffed sweatshirt" is easy to make. Sew the neck and waist of a sweatshirt. Fill the shirt through the sleeves with dried beans, rice, or noodles. The student can explore the contents by placing hands and arms into the sleeves (assistance may be needed for placement). Consider the size of the shirt in relation to the size of the student. We recommend supervision during this activity. When the shirt is not in use, fastening rubber bands around the cuffs will prevent spilling the contents.

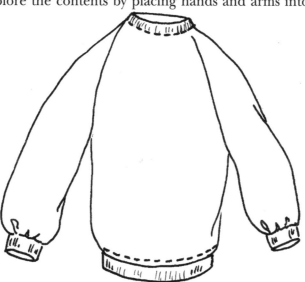

Sew closed along dashed lines at collar and cuffs

Weighted Vests

Using weighted garments provides proprioceptive input and often can reduce an individual's level of arousal during demanding times (such as transition and seatwork). **Always consult a trained therapist when considering use of weighted materials.**

Weighted Vests

- Are not recommended for individuals who have respiratory difficulties, asthma, or who are pregnant.

- Use for twenty to thirty minutes on and at least one hour off.

- Individualize weight to each person. Start with small amounts of evenly distributed weight and add or reduce weight as appropriate. Size is not always an indication of weight needs. Vest manufacturers appear to recommend up to approximately 5% of the individual's weight. Adding more than 10% of a person's body weight is cause for orthopedic concern.

- Watch for drooping shoulders, difficulty in moving, excessive mellowness, and lethargy, all symptoms of possible difficulty.

Fabricate vests from hunting, fishing, or fashion vests. Add "pockets" (two on front and two on back) for weights. Try cutting sleeves off a zippered sweatshirt, using the material to fabricate pockets for the weights. However, this may not be suitable for heavier weights, due to stretching.

Weights can be dried beans, washers, or fishing weights placed in small, sealed plastic bags or sewn fabric bags. Distribute the weights evenly. Position the pockets for weights so that they do not rest on the hips or legs when the individual is seated.

Use weighted vests with caution for individuals who may remove or mouth small objects.

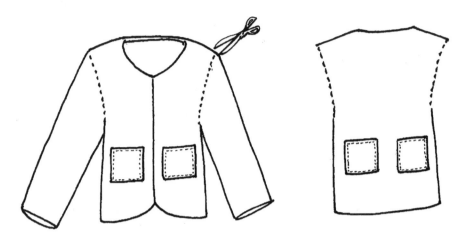

Cut off sleeves and use the sleeve material to make four pockets to hold weights. Sew two pockets on front of vest and two pockets on back. Close with Velcro® or basted stitch.

Oral Box

The two types of oral sensory dysfunction, "hyper" (over-registration/defensive) and "hypo" (under-registration), result in mild to severe oral or feeding difficulties. Using an "oral box" can provide supplies at a therapist's fingertips and yet meet the child's specific needs.

An "oral box" provides individuals with edibles and nonedibles to assist with oral-seeking behaviors and can decrease a person's level of arousal.

Fill the oral box with some of the following items: gum, gummy bears, Tootsie Rolls®, suckers, rocket suckers (promote lip rounding), squeeze pops (can place gel in specific spots), licorice, pretzels, graham crackers, edible bubbles, crunchy or chewy foods (promote oral strength), glycerin swabs, Nuk, whistles, bubbles, pacifiers, and various straws. The list on the next page classifies suggested foods for children and adults with oral sensory dysfunction based on their effect on arousal level.

Create a therapeutic oral box from a fisherman's tackle box. Large, two-level tackle boxes are especially useful. A number of items can be stored in the lower level of the box, and items specific for the individual being treated can be placed on the upper level. Very small tackle boxes can be specific for an individual and used as needed or recommended throughout the day.

Food Suggestions for Children and Adults

Arousing	Calming
Crunchy	Chewy
dried cereal	raisins
apples, raw vegetables	bagels
crackers, pretzels	fruity chews
popcorn	licorice
granola bars	
Spicy foods	Sweet foods
Cold temperature	Warm temperature
drinks, ice chips,	hot chocolate drinks
Popsicles®	

Example of a Fact Sheet

Pamela's Strengths and Challenges

General Information

Pamela turns nine in March. In reading, she has almost completed first grade, and in math, she is 80% complete in her kindergarten curriculum. Her overall knowledge is strong in some areas and weak in others. Do not underestimate her knowledge based on what she says. We have found she knows a lot more than we realize!

Pamela does not seek to make friends, but she does not avoid children. Many adults with autism report years later that they wanted to make friends but had no idea how to do it or how to fit in with other children.

Pamela's Strengths

Pamela has an excellent visual memory—a skill that helped her to learn how to read. Her ability to read has allowed her to learn language and math more easily. Pamela possesses excellent computer skills, and she can learn from computer software. Pamela enjoys art activities and writing. She recently became interested in drawing pictures.

She can state her needs and ask simple questions. She also likes describing what she's doing when she is playing. Pamela is very observant and is very aware of events around her. She enjoys many activities in her free time beyond watching videos. Her activities include play, imagination, and reading.

Pamela's Challenges

Pamela has a hard time listening and remembering what she hears—this makes it difficult for her to learn language. She has not learned to hold a conversation. She is hypersensitive to the sounds made by fluorescent lights. She is terrified of the sounds of elevators.Some of her sound-hypersensitivity causes her to cry and tantrum.

Tips for Interacting with Pamela

Talking

Talk directly to Pamela and, if necessary, get down to her physical level and get closer to her. Make eye contact to get her attention, but don't require it all the time (some people with autism can use either sight or hearing, not both). Make short, simple statements with positive wording (tell her what to do rather than saying "stop it").

Avoid double meanings, jokes, sarcasm, etc. because people with autism tend to take these literally. Allow her time to process your request and her response (counting to five helps). Provide her with visual cues, such as gestures, writing, or drawing.

Behavior

When it comes to autism, view behavior (even negative) as a form of communication. One goal is to teach Pamela to use positive behaviors to obtain her needs. Imagine yourself surrounded by loud noises and chaos. Then imagine that you are unable to speak. How are you going to let the world know that you are overwhelmed?

Imagine yourself in situations where you are bored, frustrated, or just do not feel like doing anything, but do not know how to express your feelings. When Pamela starts to tantrum, this is what she is probably experiencing! Rather than viewing a tantrum as bratty behavior, ask yourself what Pamela is trying to say.

Look at Her Strengths

Pamela is very knowledgeable about many subjects. She will not be able to give long, detailed information, but she can answer simple questions. When asking questions, be specific (e.g., "What month?" is better than "When?"). When asking a yes/no question, cue her that it is a question: "Was George Washington born in December? Yes or no."

Let her show her thoughts by drawing pictures. Pamela loves talking about calendars, seasons, weather, animals, drawing, etc. She also loves questions in the form of riddles: "I was born in February. My picture is on a quarter. I cut down a cherry tree when I was a boy. Who am I?"

Example of a Home/Classroom Handout

Student: _____   Date: _____

Sensory Break Suggestions

Anticipate the student's level of arousal, as this can impact task attention. Provide sensory breaks as needed. Be aware that one's stress level may elevate as demands compound and stressors in the environment build.

Sensory input is labeled Vestibular (V), Proprioceptive (P), Tactile (T), Visual (Vis), Olfactory (O), or Auditory (A)

Classroom Breaks That Provide Movement

A   Office "jobs" (V, P)

  • Pushing chairs under desks

  • Erasing boards

  • Using hole punchers, pencil sharpeners, staplers

  • Carrying, stacking, and sorting classroom books

B   Running office errands

C   Classroom Life Skills Tasks

  • Cooking tasks (T, V, P)

  • Setting/clearing table (V)

- Emptying trash (V, P)

- Crushing cans (P)

- Washing/wiping windows (V, P)

D   Exercise (V, P)

- Exercise bike

- Rowing machine

- Walks/hikes/races

- Structured exercise program

- Scooter board activities

- Parachute games (incorporate partner games)

- Follow the leader (while holding on to a partner)

- Movement to music activities

Sedentary Classroom Breaks

These are also important, as sometimes movement takes more excess energy and can be arousing. Quiet times can include dimming lights and lowering voices to decrease auditory and visual stimuli.

A   Providing a "quiet corner of the world" in the classroom (or home) with minimal distractions can be a nice getaway.Incorporate various items, such as large, commercially available pillows, beanbag chairs, gliders, or rocking chairs, which provide calming proprioceptive and vestibular input.

B   Providing seating adaptations such as

*   Theratubing or theraband around the front legs of the student's chair so that she can "fidget" with her feet (V, P)

*   Add movement when on the computer by having the student sit on a large therapy ball stabilized in a shallow box (V, P)

C   Listening to music or storybooks on tape (using headsets) (P)

D   Computer activities (while on therapy ball) (V)

E   Pencil and paper activities (T)

F   Art activities (T)

G   Measuring/pouring tactile substances, such as dried beans, rice, or pasta (T)

H   Exploring a variety of scents in bottles (identify and match) (O)

I   Lotion massage (T)

General Communication Tips

For students with sensory integration difficulties, the world can be difficult to understand, with the most complex factor in the environment being "people." People are often unpredictable, loud, move too much, and touch too much. Using the following "tips" can enhance communication, decrease stress level, and improve overall function.

- Do not assume receptive language is adequate.

- Provide information in brief, clear, positive statements. Tell the student what to do rather than what not to do.

- Use visuals when possible.

- Use sign language or universal signs to facilitate better comprehension.

- Lower speech volume when speaking.

- Prepare the student by communicating what is about to happen and then providing information throughout an interaction. This not only maintains calmness but also "teaches" language.

- Provide time for response.

- Use a "singsong" voice or exaggerated inflection to gain the person's attention.

- Remember that echolalic speech or "repeated speech" may convey meaning.

- Expand communication expressions; for example, if a child names the object "ball," add "Let's play ball."

- Do not engage in excessive "talk" when a student is upset.

- Avoid sarcasm, innuendos, double meanings, and unclear statements.

- If the child is mono-channel, decrease communication while he is engaged in a challenging task. There are times when less information is better.

- Interact and relate every time you work with a student.

References & Recommended Readings

Anderson, Joanna M. 1999. Sensory Motor Issues in Autism. San Antonio: Psychological Corp.

Attwood, Tony, and Temple Grandin. 2000. "Tony and Temple – Face-to-Face." Autism/Asperger's Digest (January-February).

Attwood, Tony. 1999. Asperger's Syndrome: A Guide for Parents and Professionals. Arlington, TX: Future Horizons. Videocassette.

——. 1998. Asperger's Syndrome: A Guide for Parents and Professionals. London: Jessica Kingsley.

——. 1997. "The Early Diagnosis of Autism." The Morning News (spring).

Ayres, A. Jean. 1979. Sensory Integration and the Child. Los Angeles: Western Psychological.

Baker, G., and K. Gester. 1977. "Vestibular Stimulation with Autistic and Schizophrenic Children." Alabama Journal of Medical Sciences 14: 434-435.

Ball, Donna. 1999. "Visual Supports: Helping Children With Autism." OT Practice (October).

Baron-Cohen, Simon. 1997. Mindblindness: An Essay on Theory Of Mind. Cambridge, MA: Bradford Books.

Benbow, Mary, et al. 1995. Handwriting in the Classroom; Classroom Applications for School-Based Practice. Rockville, MD: AOTA.

Beversdorf, David Q., et al. 2001. "Brief Report: Macrographia in High-Functioning Adults with Autism Spectrum Disorder." Journal of Autism and Developmental Disorders 31 (1).

Bissell, Julie, et al. 1998. Sensory Motor Handbook: A Guide for Implementing and Modifying Activities in the Classroom. Torrance, CA: Sensory Integration International.

Blanche, Erna, et al. 1995. Combining Neuro-Developmental Treatment and Sensory Integration Principles. Tucson: Therapy Skill Builders.

Bright, T., and K. Bittick. 1981. "Reduction of Self-Injurious Behavior Using Sensory Integrative Techniques." American Journal of Occupational Therapy 35: 167-72.

Butrick-Wenger, Dorothy. 1998. "Using SI Techniques With Adults With Head Injury." OT Practice (November).

Case-Smith, Jane. 1997. "Clinical Interpretation of 'Factor Analysis on the Sensory Profile from a National Sample of Children Without Disabilities." American Journal of Occupational Therapy 51 (7): 496-499.

———. 1993. Pediatric Occupational Therapy and Early Intervention. Newton, MA: Butterworth-Heinemann.

Charlop, M.H., and J.P. Milstein. 1989. "Teaching Autistic Children Conversational Speech Using Video Modeling." Journal of Applied Behavioral Analysis 22: 275-285.

Coleman, R.S., et al. 1976. "The Effects of Florescent and Incandescent Illumination upon Repetitive Behaviors in Autistic Children." Journal of Autism and Developmental Disorders 6: 157-62.

Coling, Marcia Cain. 1995. Developing Integrated Programs: A Transdisciplinary Approach for Early Intervention. Tucson: Therapy Skill Builders.

Courchesne, E., et al. 1994. "Parietal Damage and Narrow 'Spotlight' Spatial Attention." Journal of Cognitive Neuroscience (January).

Daw, Jennifer Cantello. 2001. "A Blueprint for Learning!" Autism/Asperger's Digest (May-June).

Dellacecca, Patricia, et.al. 1997. "Creating Communication Boards and Displays." Closing the Gap 15 (6).

Durand, V.M. 1988. "Motivation Assessment Scale." Dictionary of Behavioral Assessment Techniques. Eds. M. Hersen and A.S. Bellack. New York: Pergamon.

Edelson, Stephen M. n.d. "Physical Exercise and Autism." Salem, OR: Center for the Study of Autism. Retrieved from www.autism.org/exercise.html.

Ermer, Julie, and Winnie Dunn. 1998. "The Sensory Profile: A Discriminate Analysis of Children with and without Disabilities." American Journal of Occupational Therapy 52 (4): 283-289.

Ernsperger, Lori, and Tania Stegen-Hanson. 2004. Just Take A Bite. Arlington, TX: Future Horizons.

Ernsperger, Lori. 2003. Keys to Success for Teaching Students with Autism. Arlington, TX: Future Horizons.

Escalona, A., T. Field, R. Singer-Strunck, C. Cullen, and K. Hartshorn. 2001. "Brief Report: Improvements in the Behavior of Children with Autism Following Massage Therapy." Journal of Autism and Developmental Disorders 31 (5) (October).

Favell, J.E., and J.F. McGimsey. 1982. "Treatment of Self-Injury by Providing Alternate Sensory Activities." Analysis and Intervention in Developmental Disabilities 2: 83-104.

Feldman, Jean. 1995. Transition Time. Beltsville, MD: Grypon House.

Field T., et al. 1997. "Brief Report: Autistic Children's Attentiveness and Responsivity Improve After Touch Therapy." Journal of Autism and Developmental Disorders 27 (3).

Filipek, Pauline A., et al. 1999. "The Screening and Diagnosis of Autistic Spectrum Disorders." Journal of Autism and Developmental Disorders 28 (6).

Fink, Barbara. 1993. Sensory Motor Integration Activities. Tucson: Therapy Skill Builders.

Fouse, Beth. 1996. Creating a Win-Win IEP for Students with Autism. Arlington, TX: Future Horizons.

Fouse, Beth, and Maria Wheeler. 1997. A Treasure Chest of Behavioral Strategies. Arlington, TX: Future Horizons.

Freeman, Sabrina, and Lorelei Dake. 1996. Teach Me Language. Langley. BC, Canada: SKF Books.

Frost, Lori, and Andrew Bondy. 1985. The Picture Exchange Communication System. Newark: Pyramid Educational Consultants.

Gilliam, James. 1995. Gilliam Autism Rating Scale. Austin: Pro-Ed.

Grandin, Temple. 1986. Emergence: Labeled Autistic. Novato, CA: Arena Press.

———. 1998. Sensory Challenges & Answers. Arlington, TX: Future Horizons. Videocassette.

———. 1995. Thinking in Pictures. New York: Doubleday.

Gray, Carol. 1994. Comic Strip Conversations. Arlington, TX: Future Horizons.

———. 1994. The New Social Story Book: Illustrated Edition. Arlington, TX: Future Horizons.

Greenspan, Stanley, and Serena Wieder. 1998. The Child with Special Needs. Reading, PA: Addison-Wesley.

Haack, Laurel, and Mary Haldy. 1996. "Making It Easy: Adapting Home and School Environments." OT Practice (November).

Hanschu, Bonnie, and Judith Reisman. 1992. Sensory Integration Inventory-Revised for Individuals with Developmental Disabilities. Stillwater, MN: PDP Press.

Held, R., and A. Hein. 1963. "Movement -Produced Stimulation in the Development of Visually Guided Behavior." Journal of Comparative and Physiological Psychology 56 (5): 872-876

Henderson, Anne, and Charlane Pehoski. 1995. Hand Function in the Child. St. Louis: Mosby Press.

Hirsch, Nancy, and Brenda Smith Myles. 1996. "The Use of a Pica Box in Reducing Pica Behavior in a Student with Autism." Focus on Autism and Other Developmental Disabilities 11 (4).

Hodgdon, Linda A. 1995. Visual Strategies for Improving Communication. Troy, MI: Quirk Roberts.

Joe, Barbara E. 1998. "Are Weighted Vests Worth Their Weight?" OT Week (21 May).

Johnson, Anne Marie, and Jackie Susnik. 1997. Social Skills Stories: Functional Picture Stories for Readers and Nonreaders K-12. Solana Beach, CA: Mayer Johnson.

Kashman, Nancy, et al. 2000. "The Use of Videos in Assessment and Intervention of Children with Autism." OT Practice (July).

Kientz, Mary Alhage, and Winnie Dunn. 1997. "A Comparison of the Performance of Children with and Without Autism on the Sensory Profile." American Journal of Occupational Therapy 51 (7): 530-537.

King, L.J. 1991. "Sensory Integration: An Effective Approach to Therapy and Education." Autism Research Review International 5 (2).

Klein, Marsha Dunn, and Tracy Delaney. 1994. Feeding and Nutrition for the Child with Special Needs. Tucson: Therapy Skill Builders.

Korsten, Jane, et al. 1989. Every Move Counts: Sensory-Based Communication Techniques. Tucson: Therapy Skill Builders.

Kranowitz, Carol. 2003. The Out-of-Sync Child Has Fun. New York: Perigee.

Kranowitz, Carol. 2001. The Out-of-Sync Child. Las Vegas: Sensory Resources. Videocassette.

Kranowitz, Carol. 1998. The Out-of-Sync Child. New York: Perigee.

Krauss, K. 1987. "The Effects of Deep Pressure Touch on Anxiety." American Journal of Occupational Therapy 41 (8): 366-73.

Lovaas, O.I., L. Schreibman, R. Koegel, and R. Rehm. 1971. "Selective responding by autistic children to multiple sensory input." Journal of Abnormal Psychology 77: 211-222.

Luscre, Deanna M., and David B. Center. 1996. "Procedures for Reducing Dental Fear in Children with Autism." Journal of Autism and Developmental Disorders 26 (5).

Mora, Janet, and Nancy Kashman. 1997. "Strategies for Sensory Integration." Advance for Speech-Language Pathologists & Audiologists (15 December) (reprinted in Advance for Occupational Therapists; 27 April 1998).

—— 1997. "Teaming and the Use of Sensory Integration Strategies in Early Intervention." Jenison, MI: The Morning News (spring).

Morris, Suzanne Evans, and Marsha Dunn Klein. 2001. Pre-Feeding Skills, 2nd Edition. Tucson: Therapy Skill Builders.

Motola, Beth. 1996. "Using the SI Inventory for Individuals with Developmental Disabilities." Advance for Occupational Therapists (4 March).

Oetter, Patricia, et al. 1995. M.O.R.E. Integrating the Mouth with Sensory and Postural Functions. Stillwater, MN: PDP Press.

Parks, Stephanie. 1992. Inside HELP: Hawaii Early Learning Profile. Palo Alto, CA: VORT Corp.

Quill, Kathleen Ann. 1995. Teaching Children With Autism: Strategies to Enhance Communication and Socialization. New York: Delmar.

Reese, Pam Britton, and Nena Challenner. 2001. Autism and PDD: Adolescent Social Skills Lessons Set. East Moline, IL: LinguiSystems.

Restall, Gayle, and Joyce Magill-Evans. 1994. "Play and Preschool Children with Autism." The American Journal of Occupational Therapy 48 (2).

Richman, Linda. 1987. This Is the One I Want. Solana Beach, CA: Mayer Johnson.

Roley Susanne Smith, Erna Imperatore Blanche, and Roseann C. Schaaf, Eds. 2001. Understanding The Nature of Sensory Integration with Diverse Populations. San Antonio: Therapy Skill Builders.

Sheets, Lana, and Mary Wirkus. 1997 "Everyone's Classroom." Closing the Gap (April-May).

Shilling, D.L., et al. 2003. "Classroom seating for Children with Attention Deficit Hyperactivity Disorder: Therapy Balls Versus Chairs." The American Journal of Occupational Therapy 57 (5) (September/October).

Simpson, Richard L., and Brenda Smith Myles. 1998. Educating Children and Youths with Autism: Strategies for Effective Practice. Austin: Pro-Ed.

Tanta, K, et al. 2000. "Transitioning Young Children to School-Based Services: Perspectives from an Early Intervention Program." School System Special Interest Quarterly (March).

Vig, Susan, and E. Jedrysek. 1999. "Autistic Features in Young Children with Significant Cognitive Impairment: Autism or Mental Retardation?" Journal of Autism and Developmental Disorders 29 (6).

Wetherby, Amy M. and Barry M. Prizant. n.d. Autism Spectrum Disorders: Need-Based Service Delivery for Young Children. Rockville, MD: American Speech-Language-Hearing Association.

Wilbarger, Pat, and J.L. Wilbarger. 1991. Sensory Defensiveness in Children Aged 2-12: An Intervention Guide for Parents and Other Caretakers. Santa Barbara, CA: Avanti Educational Programs.

Williams, Donna. 1994. Nobody Nowhere: The Extraordinary Biography of An Autistic. New York: Perennial.

———. 1996. Autism: An Inside/Outside Approach. London: Jessica Kingsley.

Wise, Molly. 1997. "Packing Your Simple Technology Survival Kit." Closing the Gap (February-March).

Wiznitzer, Max. 1997. "Why Can't My Child Sleep?: Sleep Disturbances in Autism." Jenison, MI: The Morning News (spring).

Zihni, et al. 2000. "The AZ Method: The Use of Video Techniques to Develop Language Skills in Autistic Children." Autism/Asperger's Digest (January-February).

Recommended Assessment Sources

Beery, Keith E., Norman A. Buktenica, and Natasha A. Beery. 2004. The Beery-Buktenica Developmental Test of Visual-Motor Integration, 5th Edition (Beery VMI). Minneapolis: Pearson Assessments.

Brown, Catanna, and Winnie Dunn. Infant/Toddler Sensory Profile. 2002. San Antonio: Psychological Corp.

Brownell, Rick, ed. 2000. Expressive One-Word Picture Vocabulary Test (EOWPVT-2000), 2000 Edition. Hydesville, CA: Psychological and Educational Publications, Inc.

Bzoch, Kenneth R., Richard League, and Virginia L. Brown. 2003. Receptive-Expressive Emergent Language Scale, 3rd Edition (REEL-3). Hydesville, CA: Psychological and Educational Publications.

Coster, Wendy J., et al. 1998. School Function Assessment (SFA). San Antonio: Psychological Corp.

D'Eugenio, Diane, and Martha S. Moersch, eds. 1981. Developmental Programming for Infants and Young Children, Volumes 4 and 5 – Preschool Assessment and Application. Ann Arbor: The University of Michigan Press.

Dunn, Lloyd M., and Leota M. Dunn. 1997. Peabody Picture Vocabulary Test, 3rd Edition (PPVT-III). Circle Pines, MN: AGS Publishing.

Folio, M .Rhonda, and Rebecca R. Fewell. 2000. Peabody Developmental Motor Scale-2nd Edition (PDMS-2). Austin: Pro-Ed.

Hedrick, Dona Lea, Elizabeth M. Prather, and Annette R. Tobin. 2000. Sequenced Inventory of Communication Development-Revised (SICD-R). Los Angeles: Western Psychological.

Parks, Stephanie. Hawaii Early Learning Profile (HELP®). 1999. Palo Alto, CA: VORT Corp.

Reisman, Judith E., and Bonnie Hanschu. 1992. Sensory Integration Inventory-Revised for Individuals with Developmental Disabilities. (SII-R). Stillwater, MN: PDP Press.

Rogers, Sally J., et al, eds. 1981. Developmental Programming for Infants and Young Children, Volume 2 – Early Intervention Developmental Profile, Revised. Ann Arbor: The University of Michigan Press.

Zimmerman, Irla Lee, Violette G. Steiner, and Roberta E. Pond. 2002. Preschool Language Scale, 4th Edition (PLS-4). San Antonio: Psychological Corp.

Recommended Resources

Anything's Possible, Inc. (Special Kids Speech & Skill Development Resources), 1863 N Farwell Ave., Milwaukee, WI 53202; Phone: (800) KIDS-153; www.specialkids1.com (commercial videos for skill development)

Autism Society of America, 7910 Woodmont Avenue, Suite 300, Bethesda, MD 20814; Telephone: (800) 3AUTISM; www.autism-society.org

Autism Research Institute, 4182 Adams Avenue, San Diego, CA 92116; Phone: (619) 563-6840; www.autism.com/ari (Bernard Rimland, Ph.D.)

Center for the Study of Autism, P.O. Box 4538, Salem, OR 97302; www.autism. org (Internet articles and research)

Closing The Gap, PO Box 68, Henderson, MN 56044; Phone: (507) 248-3294; www.closingthegap.com (Provides information about computer technology in special education and rehabilitation)

Ellison Education Equipment, 25862 Commercentre Dr., Lake Forest, CA 92630; Phone: (800) 253-2238; www.ellison.com (Ellison Press Equipment)

Enabling Devices, 385 Warburton Ave., Hastings-on-Hudson, NY 10706; Phone: (800) 832-8697; www.enablingdevices.com (motivational toys, switches)

Future Horizons, Inc. 721 W. Abram St., Arlington, TX 76013; Phone: (800) 489-0727; Fax: (817) 277-2270; www.futurehorizons-autism.com; Email: Info@futurehorizons-autism.com (Provides national conferences and books on the autism spectrum; also publishes the Autism-Asperger's Digest, a bi-monthly magazine)

Gary Lamb Music (Kagan Publishing), PO Box 72008, San Clemente, CA 92673; Phone: (800) 772-7701; www.garylamb.com; Email: questions@garylamb. com (Music with 60 beats per minute)

Glaser, Tammy; Email: 798@earthlink.net (Parent: source of information for teaching strategies, alternative therapies including nutrition)

Handwriting Without Tears, 8001 MacArthur Blvd Cabin John, MD 20818; Phone: (301) 263-2700; www.hwtears.com (Handwriting program by Jan Olsen)

Intellitools, Inc., 1720 Corporate Cir., Petaluma, CA 94954; Phone: (800) 899-6687; www.intellitools.com (Intellikeys, Intellitalk software)

Journal of Autism and Developmental Disorders, published by Human Sciences Press; available online through Kluwer Online Journals: www.kleweronline.com (Information about current research in the field of autism)

MAAP Services, Inc., P.O. Box 524, Crown Point, IN 46307; Phone: (219) 662-1311; www.maapservices.org (More Advanced Autistic People; provides a newsletter and other family services)

Mayer-Johnson LLC, PO Box 1579, Solana Beach, CA 92075; Phone: (800) 588-4548, Fax: (858) 550-0449; www.mayer-johnson.com (Boardmaker software)

The Morning News/The Jenison Autism Journal (now known as Autism Spectrum Quarterly with Dr. Diane Twachtman-Cullen, Editor), Phone: (860) 635-2906; www.asquarterly.com (Articles for, by, and about individuals with autism spectrum disorders)

PDP Products, 14524 61st Court N, Stillwater, MN 55082 Phone: (612) 439-8865; www.pdppro.com (books, oral equipment)

Playaway Toy Company, PO Box 247, Bear Creek, WI 54922 Phone: (888) 752-9929; www.playawaytoy.com (Indoor therapy swings and attachments)

Pocket Full of Therapy, PO Box 174, Morganville, NJ 07751 Phone: (800) PFOT-124; www.pfot.com (sensory equipment)

Sensory Resources LLC, 2500 Chandler Ave., Ste. 3, Las Vegas, NV 89120; Phone: (888) 357-5867. Fax (702) 891-8899; www.SensoryResources.com; Email: Info@SensoryResources.com (Provides national conferences and publications on sensory integration disorders)

Southpaw Enterprises, PO Box 1047, Dayton, OH 45401; Phone: (800) 228-1698; www.southpawenterprises.com (sensory equipment, weighted and "huggy" vests)

SPD Network, sponsored by the KID Foundation, 1901 W Littleton Blvd., Littleton, CO 80120; Phone: 303-794-1182; www.spdnetwork.org (Sponsors a Resource Directory that lists doctors, therapists, and other service providers experienced in working with people with sensory processing disorder)

Therapro, Inc., 225 Arlington St., Framingham, MA 01702; Phone: (800) 257-5376, Fax: (800) 268-6624; www.theraproducts.com (oral/ sensory equipment)

Contact the Authors: Nancy Kashman and Janet Mora: janetnancy@aol.com

Index

A

activities 39
  brushing 89
  exercise/group sports 86
  fine motor 85
  gardening 86
  home 90
    bath time 90
    bedtime 91
    hygiene/grooming 90
  horiculture 86
  massage 88
  mummy game 89
  obstacle course 84
  racetrack play 83
  sock massage 89
  tactile 91
    art and finger painting 94
    ball play 95
    cooking 95
    homemade play dough 93
    pouring 92
    putty and Play-Doh 92
    sticker play 94
    "stuffed sweatshirt" 91
    water related 93
  thera-band 85
  towel rocking/pulling 83
  visual
    flashlight games 96
    handwriting 96
    mirror play 96
  washing machine 81
adults & older children 105
  food suggestions 129
  proprioceptive & vestibular activities
    can crushing 105
    Ellison LetterMachine 105
    exercise & group sports 106
    household & office chores 106
  tactile activities 108
    art activities 108
    sorting & categorizing 108
    water activities 109
Asperger's syndrome 9, 27, 152
assessment 47, 50

assorted balls 109
Attwood, Dr. Tony 27
auditory system 27, 32
autism 9, 11, 151
autism spectrum disorders 15
Ayres, Dr. A. Jean 11

B

behavior
  repetative 78
  self-abusive 34
  self-stimulating 34, 78
  sterotypic 34

C

case studies 73, 147
cerebral palsy 9, 11, 155
childhood disintegrative disorder 152
classroom
  sensory breaks 173
classroom & home chores 87
communication 14, 48
  communication boards 139
  general tips 177
  interventions 135
    with mild difficulties 134
    with moderate difficulties 133
    with severe difficulties 131
  picture exchange 137
  skills development 131
  visual or photo book 139
environment
  "corner of the world" 63
creative cards enterprise 111

D

deep pressure 24
disorders with autistic features 153
dog biscuit enterprise 110
Down syndrome 9, 11, 155
dress-up 94
dyspraxia
  oral 49

E

enterprise activities 109
environment 52, 53
  additional strategies 63
  effects on arousal level 53, 56
  guide to assessment 157
  lighting 60
  room organization 60
  tactile and proprioceptive input 61
  temperature & odors 62
  vestibular input 60
  visual supports 68
    bulletin boards 71
    color coding 71
    labels & signs 70
    lists 70
    schedules & calendars 69
    sensory "cheat sheet" 70
    visual markers 73
    visual routines 69
    visual rules 73
equipment & supplies
  contact paper 81
  Dycem 65, 128
  glider 65
  hammock 65
  inner tubes 65
  large grip utensils 128
  nosey cup 128
  Nuk massage brush 127
  "oral box" 127, 167
  playground equipment 83
  play dough (homemade) 93
  portable ball bag 80
  rocking chair 65
  slant board 98
  sports cup 128
  stuffed pants 64, 161
  stuffed sweatshirt 163
  swim noodles 64
  T-stools 64
  Thera-Band 65
  therapy ball 64
  weighted 101
    backpack 103
    blankets 102
    body sock 103
    collar 103
    foot patch 103
    hand patch 103
    huggy vest 103
    lap pocket 102
    toys and materials 84
    vests 101, 165
    weighted sock 102
  weighted utensils 128
execution 23

F

food suggestions 129
fragile X 153

G

gravitational insecurity 20
grooming 25

H

handwriting 96
  adaptations 97, 100
  attention suggestions 100
  computer adaptations 101
  copying 100
  spacing and line usage 100
hyper-responsive 15
hyperlexia 154

I

ideation 22
informational tools 120
  daily communication log 121
  digital photos 122
  fact sheet 121, 169
  home/classroom handout 122
  homework calendar 122
  information poster 121
  transitional photo book 120
internal eyes 22, 35
intervention 77
  approach 39, 41
  "sabotage" 79
  treatment stategy 78, 80

L

Landau-Kleffner syndrome 153
language
  expressive 15
  receptive 15, 48
learning 40
  environment 55

M

monochanneling 15
motivational toys 96

N

neurofibromatosis 153

O

olfactory system 29, 32
oral & feeding 24
  difficulties 30
  equipment 128
  food suggestions 128, 168
  interventions 125
  oral box 167
  proprioceptive/tactile 126
overregistration 20, 24, 30, 31

P

pervasive developmental disorder (PDD) 9, 152
Picture Exchange Communication System (PECS) 132
planning 22
postural insecurity 21
posture 68
Prader-Willi syndrome 154
praxis 17
prompts
  hierarchy 38
  motor 38
  prompt dependency 35
  verbal 38
proprioceptive system 12, 22

R

Rett syndrome 152

reverse chaining 36

S

seating, alternative 63, 161
self-care skills 25, 28, 34
senses 12
sensory breaks 173
sensory "cheat sheet" 69
sensory defensiveness 33, 34
sensory integration 11
Sensory Integration Disorders 151
sensory integration disorders 15
sensory motor
  evaluation 50
sound 57
stereotypic vocalizations 16
superhearing 27

T

tactile defensiveness 24
tactile system 24
teaming
  benefits 43
  case studies 147
tests, standardized 47
transitions & informational tools 117
treatment
  cycle 42
tuberous sclerosis 154

U

underregistration 20, 26, 30, 31

V

vestibular system 12, 19
videos 141
visuals 136
visual system 29, 32, 58

W

Wilbarger protocol 89
Williams syndrome 154
writing 23, 25